The ECONOMIC STORM

Understand It, Survive It, Make Money When It Passes

LANE J. MENDELSOHN

MARKETPLACE BOOKS®
GLENELG, MARYLAND

TRA

SEC

ADE

RETS

ISBN: 1-59280-380-6
ISBN 13: 978-1-59280-380-4

Printed in the United States of America.

CONTENTS

FOREWORD

THE "AVERAGE" INVESTOR AND THE PERFECT STORM

BY VAN K. THARP, PH.D.

I recently received an email from someone who said, "Van, I really appreciate your work, but I don't want to spend a lot of time on trading. I'm just an average investor who wants to invest in mutual funds and maybe make a decision several times each year. And I'm probably like 95% of the other investors out there." This sort of email comes to me all too frequently. And the plea is, "Tell me what to do! I don't want to spend a lot of time or do a lot of work because I'm just an average investor."

Well, let's say you are an educated professional. You have a MBA and you earn about $120,000 per year. Each year you manage to save about $10,000 of your salary after taxes; after 25 years you've saved a nest egg of about $600,000 and you retire. Or perhaps you've only saved $100,000 after ten years, and you know you'll have to do a lot better to be able to retire at the same income level. Either way, this information applies to you. And if you don't make a six-figure income and only have a small nest egg, then this information is even more pertinent.

Henry Moreno had retired in 2003. He had done well during his working years and had a retirement income of $7,000 per month, including his Social Security. That was a little over half of his working salary, but he also had saved about $650,000 as a nest egg for emergencies. He still owed about $350,000 on his house, with monthly payments of $3,070 per month. Henry and his wife debated a lot about whether or not they should pay off the mortgage with their savings. They'd still have about $300,000 left in cash if they did, and their monthly expenses would be cut in half.

Henry had lost about 30% of his retirement nest egg during the market crash from 2000 to 2003. However, in 2003 the market was going up. Henry figured the worst was over, and he could probably make 10% per year on his money. That would give them an additional $5,000 per month for spending, which more than covered his mortgage payment. Henry had an advanced degree in civil engineering, and, as far as he was concerned, investing wasn't rocket science. Yes, he was an average investor, but he'd do well in the market because he was a smart guy. Chances are, he thought, he could be better than average and get his account back up to a million dollars (like it was before the 2000 crash).

Henry made the mistake that many people make. He'd spent nearly eight years learning his profession and much of his life staying on top of it. He could build a bridge that could weather the worst of storms and the heaviest of traffic. Henry thought he probably could outsmart most market professionals and make at least 10% each year in his retirement. All he had to do, he assumed, was research a little, pick the right stocks, and just hold on. And he knew that he could do that.

Henry was now 68 years old. His total education in the market consisted of reading three or four books on how to pick the right stocks, plus a best-selling book about Warren Buffett. He also watched the financial news regularly, so he was sure he could make his fortune. And he read *Investor's Business Daily* and the *Financial Times* each day, so he felt informed.

From 2003 through 2005, Henry did okay. He made about $40,000 each year and he and his wife spent about half of that. Thus, at the beginning of 2008, Henry's account was worth about $720,000. But Henry was not ready for the perfect financial storm that was about to hit the economy throughout the world. He had enough training to build a bridge that could withstand any weather, but he didn't have the training to build a trading system that could withstand any sort of financial downpour. In fact, Henry didn't even have a trading system.

By September 30, 2008, the stock market was down more than 40% for the year, and Henry's account was down 35%—it was now worth about $468,000. If he paid off his house now, it would take most of his assets. And when the bailout bill passed, he watched the market fall by triple-digit declines each day. Henry was really worried as his account balance dropped below $400,000.

The financial media said stocks would soon be a bargain. "Don't sell unless you need the money." Didn't they realize that by that standard of just invest and hold, he was down

60% from his equity high in 2000? In fact, Henry now needed to make 70% on his money just to break even on the year, and he was struggling to make 10% per year.

What's the bottom line here? Henry spent eight years getting his education to become a good engineer. Yet, he treats the investing process like anyone can do it. It's similar to walking into a hospital and asking to operate on someone's brain without any training. You can't do that in the hospital, but it's easy to do in the market. In the hospital, it would mean someone's life. But when you do it in the market, it means the death of your account.

To trade or invest successfully, you must get the education required to do so. And that's well illustrated by Lane Mendelsohn's *The Economic Storm*. Big banks don't understand risk because they think it has to do with performance volatility, not how much they can lose. Thus, as Mendelsohn points out, when the government repealed the 1933 Glass Steagall Bank Act, it opened the door for banks to now prove that they had learned nothing in the early 1930s. At that time, they didn't understand risk and they still don't understand it. Furthermore, the repeal of Glass Steagall allowed banks to increase their leverage dramatically just to show how little they understood risk. Ironically, they would never allow you to invest like that if you had a brokerage account with them. As Mendelsohn says:

Glass-Steagall limited the debt-to-asset ratio for banks to 6:1. Beginning in 2000, Congress and the SEC gradually eased this restriction. In 2004, the restricting ratio dramatically jumped when Henry Paulson (then CEO of Goldman

Sachs), successfully lobbied to increase the debt-to-asset ratio considerably. When September 2008 rolled around, many of the large banks and other financial institutions had leveraged their assets to levels as high as 40:1. This unbelievable and unsustainable leveraging is the single, most profound reason we are where we are today.

And what did they leverage as high as 40:1? Collateralized Debt Obligations, which contained subprime mortgages that had a huge potential for failure because they were loans made to people who could not afford them, just because the U.S. government said it was okay to make such loans.

In *The Economic Storm,* Mendelsohn goes on to lay out all of the events that came together to make this a storm like no other we have ever seen. In fact, I was not aware of all of them myself until I read this book.

In all of my years as a trading coach, I've discovered that there are so many pitfalls that investors and traders can encounter that even the best thought-out plans usually don't include everything. As a result, you need a trading methodology that protects you should unforeseen events occur. You need to control your emotions that might keep you away from your discipline—with fear and greed, as Mendelsohn points out, being two of the major ones.

Ask yourself the following questions:

1. Do you understand the big picture as Mendelsohn has described it in this book? If not, then be sure you do.

2. Are you treating trading/investing like a business? Have you prepared for it like a business?

3. Do you have a strategy to guide you when you trade/invest? In this book, Mendelsohn points to five major rules that should be part of any strategy.

4. Do you have a way of knowing when the storm is over? Mendelsohn does.

There are numerous other questions that you probably should ask yourself and that you'll learn about as you get the proper education that is necessary to survive in these markets.

Let's say you've spent eight years learning how to build a bridge that would survive any storm. And for that you are paid a six-figure salary. Now, you expect to make a six-figure salary in the market without getting a similar education in trading/investing? You know what it takes to build a bridge that can weather any storm, but you are willing to build an economic bridge to the future without such training.

I've been teaching investors and traders how to ask themselves the right questions for nearly thirty years, and I've been associated with TraderPlanet (and its predecessor) for the last four years. We both believe in the same thing: If you want to make a good salary in the markets, you need the proper training and education.

Here is what you need to do: Don't accept the notion that you are just an average investor. You create your own results. Do your results right now come from playing a game with your money with no training at all in how to play that game?

If you trade for yourself, you need to follow the guidelines contained in this book. If you do not trade for yourself and have professionals trading for you, do you realize they must be 95% invested even in a falling market? They get paid 1%-2% of the value of the assets they have under management. They get paid even if you lose money. And remember, even traders that you might have considered to be the most professional (those in big banks) have already proven that they don't understand risk and don't know to manage it.

You know what it takes to overcome the gray skies in your profession, but are you willing to get the proper education you need to weather the economic storm?

Van K. Tharp, Ph.D.
President, The Van Tharp Institute

PREFACE

Wisdom is difficult for young people to grasp. I know because I am just starting to understand the meaning of the things my parents taught me as a young man, especially as they relate to hard economic times. For example, as a small boy, my mother hired me to remove weeds from our garden. She said she would pay five cents per weed pulled. Within that simple, verbal contract resided a lesson, which I learned the first time I pulled weeds for her.

Earning five cents for every weed pulled motivated me to pull as many weeds as I could as fast as I could. With a bagful of weeds in hand, I went to my mother to get my money. She looked in the bag, pushed the weeds around, looked at me and said, "Sorry, no money for these. I told you that you get a nickel for every weed you pull that still has the root ball attached. None of these have a root ball."

Looking at our financial problems today, it occurs to me that investors inside financial institutions who knew better went out and "pulled as many weeds as they could as fast as they could." In other words, the idea of making "easy" money overrode what they knew to be the correct way to do their job.

Another economic lesson I picked up as a young boy is one I learned from my father, who cut his financial teeth in the world of investing and trading. That lesson, cliché as it might be, is that this is a dog-eat-dog world, and you have to protect yourself with awareness and good choices.

When a dog barks, pay attention. If a dog bites, defend yourself. If you lack awareness and don't react to the warning signs, the dog will eat you. Regarding the economy, a dog barked back in 1999, and we did not listen. Then that dog bit in 2004, and we did not defend. Finally, the dog ate us in 2008. This will become clearer as we move through this book, but for now, understand that vigilance and defensive positioning are keys to survival and success in the investing and trading world.

The U.S. economy entered an "official" recession in December 2007. In the middle of 2009, one could argue that the economy is close to turning the corner and heading toward a recovery based on some "green shoots" sprouting. Is the economy really on the verge of recovery?

To be clear, I am not an economist, so this book is not an attempt to answer the question above. We all are, however, investors and traders. It is our job to avoid speculation and to formulate educated guesses with facts. That is how we make money. We look at reality, define and understand its parameters, and then reach for the tools we utilize to find good investments. Thus, answering the above question is irrelevant.

Specifically, the reason for this book is to help us understand this recession, so we can set up and prepare for the recovery. A predicted recovery date is not helpful. Identifying factual data that points to a recovery, tracking that data, and then ascertaining potential investments so that we might make money is helpful.

The first important piece of data that we now understand is that this economic "downturn" is not your run-of-the-mill recession. In fact, we have now accumulated economic statistics that rank this recession as one of the deepest in U.S. history. The current recession also has characteristics unlike any other in our history. For the first time, we have seen a confluence of negative events come together to form a "perfect storm," if you will. This recession arrived with the collapse of the housing market in late 2006, gained force with the associated rise in foreclosures and unemployment in 2007, and its full fury emerged in September 2008 with the announced failures of Merrill Lynch and Lehman Brothers. These announcements came amid the revelation of just how deep the liquidity and credit problems of the banking industry ran and how damaging they would become.

The housing market collapse, the stock market crash in October 2008, the buildup of deflationary fears with the collapse of the commodity bubbles (oil specifically) in late 2008, unemployment rising to levels not seen in decades, and the seeming inability of the government to stabilize the financial system with massive infusions of cash and credit added energy to what would become a full-blown economic tempest.

Thankfully, according to those "in the know," this recession is not on track to become a depression, the likes of which we have not seen since the Great Depression of the 1930s. True or not, the reality is that the global economy at this moment is in bad shape, and the future is unknown.

Within this context, we must find a way to "weather the storm." If we do this, we will maintain our balance. If we keep our balance, we can identify signs of recovery with some certainty. Once we know the economy is turning toward recovery, we can identify potential investment possibilities.

In this book, I discuss much to gain clarity and understanding. For one, I believe that to comprehend the present and to see a glimpse of the future, one must understand the past. *How did we get here? How does the current economic recession compare to past recessions? How bad is it, really?* As well, the past might show us actions to take, or not take to protect our current investments and, in some cases, simply survive. Discussing these answers in detail will help us all get and keep our footing in these turbulent times.

By understanding the origin, the characteristics, and the depth of the recession, we can evaluate the key data points that will lead us to recovery. This same information might also point to when and how the economy will recover, and what the "new" economy might look like. *Which sectors, industries, businesses will be best positioned to gain quickly in the recovery?*

Finally, this book will examine ways to financially prepare for the recovery. *How much capital should one invest early in the recovery? What might be the best allocation of that money?* I will also discuss in detail potential ways to make money early when the recovery occurs. *What trading strategies might best suit the recovery? What investment tools will help gain the needed edge for successful investing and trading?*

These are dark days, and I believe it is about as serious as it gets for investors and traders all around the globe. I have no desire to "sugar coat" the reality or paint an abstract picture. In this book, I examine the subject areas with clarity, and I resolve to give you, the reader, my best effort to help you understand, stabilize, and prepare. If there is one thing about which I am reasonably certain, it is this: Markets go up as well as down. The issue, as always, is timing, and as investors and traders, we all know that precisely timing markets is consistently impossible and potentially dangerous. A better plan is to pull back, objectively evaluate, prepare, and then step in when confidence has replaced fear and the markets are showing strength, not weakness. Objectively and widely defining this approach is the focus of this book.

INTRODUCTION

We are at war, and we need to draw upon all of our resources to fight it. The enemy threatens our way of life, our freedom, our financial prowess and, to a great degree, our ethical and moral compass. Make no mistake, this is a world war; every developed nation on the planet is now fighting and is dedicated to defeating our collective enemy.

Perhaps you might see the above as an exaggeration when I tell you the economic recession attacking the global economy is the "collective enemy." If you do, think about this: If the global economy were to collapse into a depression, we all might very well experience ten years or more of sloshing around in the mud of an economic pit. Consider the following facts.

American households lost more than $11 trillion of personal net worth in 2008. The stock market has erased several trillion dollars of that net worth just since October 2008. This value loss negatively impacts retirement plans, investment portfolios, corporate re-investment capital, traders' cash, and extremely large public and private institutions dependent on revenue generated in the stock market. If this were not enough, housing values have dropped dramatically, foreclosures have topped historic levels, and housing construction, a prime generator of the economy, has slumped to record lows.

Keep in mind the collapse of hundreds of banks across the country, the disappearance of large financial firms such as Bear Stearns and Lehman Brothers, and the government loaning to or investing in more than twenty financial institutions to the tune of trillions of dollars. Add to these issues the virtual destruction of the American automobile industry, unemployment rising to record levels, the loss of up to $1.5 trillion in annual U.S. consumer spending, and an annual budget deficit approaching $1.5 trillion.

The truth is that convincing you of the economic ills facing us in these troubled times is not necessary. No, the point of the above statistical trip through the economic haunted house is to set the stage for the discussions in the upcoming chapters.

Regarding the "war" analogy, the point of that is to set the stage for the discussion of what is truly our common and collective enemy—greed and fear. Simply put, greed is what got us here and fear is what keeps us here. Until we defeat both, we are doomed to these devastating boom-and-bust cycles.

To express just how damaging greed and fear are to economic prosperity, think of overextended consumers as junkies—people hooked on credit supplied by a dealer with a vested interest in addiction. When credit is cheap and easy to acquire, consumer-junkies buy more than they can afford, and lender-dealers lend more than they have just to keep the credit flowing. Now, tighten up that credit or, in some cases, take it away. Panic sets in, fear and anxiety become constant, and, ultimately, a simple, yet profound, realization takes hold: To get well, consumers must stop spending and lenders must stop lending. Our collective enemy is real. Greed and fear, like enemies in any war, bring about human casualties, massive destruction, and great suffering. This is the true war, and right now, we are in the middle of the havoc it wreaks.

Because of this, I take a practical and helpful look at greed and fear. I suggest that in each is a positive seed; it is only when excess takes the reins that each becomes destructive. I discuss how they both affect investors and traders and how we might curb their negative influence and support their positive possibilities. I also put forth an ideal to aspire to, a high-minded proposition that states that we all would prosper more consistently if we accepted and acted upon a simple truth: Each of us has the power to change how we view the world at any given moment in time.

Although I talk about how each of us can change our perspective, I recognize that is a tall order, especially since huge contributors to our collective lack of confidence are those ubiquitous and pervasive elements in society who make money preaching greed and selling fear. The media in general and the financial media in particular need to look closely at how they analyze and report the news.

When talking heads, financial pundits, and newscasters unabashedly push the spending addiction, bad things happen. When they dramatize the negative to attract viewers, confidence at every level falls and bubbles burst. Banks that lend to other banks stop lending. Consumers who can spend stop spending. Investors who want to invest don't because they can't see a floor. Corporations lack confidence in the future, so they lay off workers, cut spending, and reduce their profit outlook, resulting in a further rise in unemployment and a loss in investor confidence. Traders see the lack of confidence everywhere, sell short, and the markets suffer. As investors and traders, the reality is that we know more about what is really happening than most talking heads, financial pundits, and newscasters.

Just in case you thought all I want to talk about is the bad, here is the best of all information I could ever give: The economy will turn around. This is an historical fact. My goal in the chapters that follow is to demonstrate this and to pull from that historical analysis important data that points to certain signs of recovery. Once I identify those signs, I discuss what "recovery" means to us as investors and traders. Specifically, I look at potential investment areas that will naturally flow from a recovery. These potential investments exist in strong industries, strong companies, and strong sectors beaten down in the recession; in parts of the economy receiving massive expenditures of federal dollars; and in specific sectors of the "new" economy devoted to the transitions occurring in energy production and use, the manufacturing base, and in infrastructure renovations.

Simply stated, my goal is to help us all understand this unique recession, so we can set up and prepare for the recovery. Along the way to the goal, I discuss the overall nature and specific elements of this recession, how we got here, how this recession compares to other recessions, and how we might think and behave to minimize our pain and maximize our potential. I frame a perspective from which we can assess where the economy is now, and where it is going.

The ECONOMIC STORM

Understand It, Survive It, Make Money When It Passes

HOW DID WE GET HERE?

THE VALUE OF UNDERSTANDING

Clearly, the U.S. economy and the overall global economy are in trouble. History tells us that when the economy is in trouble, we should be concerned. As investors, we are in the business of making money, and when the economy is in trouble, making money becomes more difficult. However, history also tells us that no matter the depth and severity of the economic crisis, the economy will eventually recover and begin expanding and generating wealth once again. This has been the case in the past, and it is the case now. Our economy will recover. The issue is not *if*, but *when* it will recover?

The answer is unknown, and to venture a prediction about the end of this unique recession is a game played poorly by even the wisest financial gurus among us. For the money, it is better to pass on guessing when the recession will end; rather, it is in our best interest to understand the recession holistically and completely so we can prepare for the eventual recovery. Taking this perspective does several important things for us. First, and most importantly, it allows us to see the recession for what it truly is, not what the world of talking heads, pundits, and newscasters tells us it is. Understanding the recession puts the power of investing and trading in our hands, not someone else's. It allows us to make choices with an objective, clear mindset, and that is always the best way to make choices when money is at stake.

Along with not relinquishing our power, we enhance the likelihood of future trading success when we understand the true nature of this recession, as this one is beyond anything we have seen in our lifetimes and in so many ways dissimilar to the greatest economic upheaval we have faced as a nation, the Great Depression.

Understanding this recession, particularly the key elements that caused it, allows us to prepare more accurately for the eventual recovery. By understanding how we got here and the true nature of where we are, we can more readily define data points that act as signs pointing to recovery. With the same information, we can then devise tools to help us invest or trade with greater success.

The last value in understanding all we can about this recession, particularly how we got here, is that we can learn how we might see the next one coming and take appropriate steps to protect our positions and our cash.

WHAT HAPPENED?

Many have argued the collapse of the housing market is the reason banks are in this economic mess. To a large degree, this is the case, but it is not the whole story. If one looks at the macro view of this recession, it is clear that we were inevitably headed here for some time — decades, really — and that the financial meltdown beginning in September 2008 was not a result of the housing bubble bursting. Rather, it was the other way around.

It is true that the housing market collapsed because too many financially unqualified borrowers got into loans that were way beyond their means, particularly the short-term Adjustable Rate Mortgages (ARMs). These loans, known as "subprime" loans, offered initial rates way below existing market rates. Simply, the unbelievable teaser rates, the no-income qualifying, the wealth-building potential of investing in a market that was hot, and the lure to achieve the American dream of home ownership overrode both common sense and prudent financial considerations.

Anyone paying attention in 2004 could see the housing bubble fattening up. Anyone who understands financial peaks and troughs could see the sharp upward spike from 2000 to 2005 meant a soon-to-be correction and that the correction would be as sharp on the way down. Truthfully, no one seemed to care. Everyone was making money, and, after all, that is the point of investing, right? Yes, making money is the point of investing, but this notion that bubbles always have a little more room to grow is dangerous, as we have seen recently and throughout world history.

Awareness, prudence, and careful consideration are the hallmarks of successful investing. The successful investor always keeps in mind the overarching rule of investing: Protect and preserve capital, even above making money. History has shown that following this rule is the best protection against bubbles and the mania surrounding them.

Ignorant, unskilled real estate buyers caught up in the rapid flight to riches can be, to a minor degree, forgiven, but the people who run banks, whose day-in and day-out job it is to understand the realities of financial transactions, cannot. These people are, in fact, professional investors, right? Why, then, did they throw awareness, prudence, and careful consideration out the window? Why did they ignore the fundamental rule of investing: Protect and preserve capital, even above making money? Greed overwhelmed their investing principles.

OUR LESSON

Their failure is our lesson. When everyone is making money hand-over-fist, a red flag is waving. When that flag waves wildly, it is time to look closely at the fundamentals of the "boom." Underneath the flying dollars are factual numbers that tell us how inflated a bubble is and how much more inflation it can take. In this particular bubble, the rapidly expanding, low-income market for real estate in late 2004 was an intuitive sign that the bubble had little room to expand. More important, looking at the annual and quarterly financials of the top banks in 2005 would have told us clearly the bubble was stretched as tight as a drum-skin.

Intuition is good, and often a key to success, but in a case such as this, looking at the financials of the top banks would have been much more accurate than trying to figure out how many more low-income buyers remained to keep blowing air into the bubble. For anyone who cared to look at the financials of the top banks, the numbers told us the debt-to-asset ratio was not prudent, the increasing and careless investments in low-income buyers were not carefully considered, and the lack of awareness as to the pending bubble burst was stunning.

REPEALING THE BANK ACT OF 1933

The thing about market bubbles is that they often take some time to build. The housing bubble that collapsed in late 2005 had a phenomenal six-year run, beginning in 1999 with the congressional repeal of the Bank Act of 1933 (Glass–Steagall). If we want to understand how this current economic collapse began, consider this the starting point. True, a confluence of powerful influences contributed to this economic downturn, but none proved more powerful and none contributed more to the economic collapse than this act of political pandering to the financial lobby in 1999.

In the decades between 1933 and 1999, banks were highly regulated, and it is easy to see why. Greed to a careless capitalist is like heroin to a junky. Once you taste its euphoria, you want more. Thus, Congress passed this act to curb the greedy excesses that led to the U.S. banking collapse in 1933. Americans had lost confidence in a corrupt banking system, so they withdrew enough money to collapse the system. Repealing the one law that protected the banking system against the force of greed was like having a junky move in with a dealer.

REMOVING THE WALL

The repeal of Glass–Steagall had far-reaching effects for the financial industry, including removing the protective wall between commercial banking, investment banking, and other financial institutions. In effect, the law kept banks and other financial companies from doing business on Wall Street, and vice versa. One of the driving forces behind the law was the huge amount of bank failures by 1933. The nation's banking system in 1933 was chaotic. More than 11,000 banks had failed or had to merge, reducing the number of total banks by 40 per cent, from 25,000 to 14,000. The governors of several states had already closed their states' banks by March, when President Roosevelt closed all the banks in the country.

The tangled relationships in the banking industry today clearly demonstrate the resulting problem with repealing this law. The ideal that a "freed from regulation" banking industry would produce both capital and innovation to expand the economy soon turned into a frantic pace of mergers that produced behemoths, such as CitiGroup, which seemed only interested in "the deal" and growing the size of already huge companies. The emergence of such large banking companies with the goal of making money hand-over-fist produced a myriad of new leveraged products that, ultimately, would bring a stable system to its knees in less than 10 years.

INCREASED DEBT-TO-ASSET RATIOS

Repealing the 1933 law had another damaging impact on the economy. It opened the door for the Securities and Exchange Commission (SEC) to alter the restrictions on the debt-to-asset ratio for banks. Glass-Steagall limited the debt-to-asset ratio for banks to 6:1. Beginning in 2000, Congress and the SEC gradually eased this restriction. In 2004, the restricting ratio dramatically jumped when Henry Paulson (then CEO of Goldman Sachs), successfully lobbied to increase the debt-to-asset ratio considerably. When September 2008 rolled around, many of the large banks and other financial institutions had leveraged their assets to levels as high as 40:1. This unbelievable and unsustainable leveraging is the single, most profound reason we are where we are today. Banks, much like the low-income buyer, leveraged their money way beyond their means and their ability to pay it back when favorable conditions changed to unfavorable conditions.

More leveraging meant more profit, or so the thinking went. Unfortunately, more leveraging fired up the real estate market because of the rise in loan availability, which led to the enormous bubble that has since burst.

Repealing Glass-Steagall removed the protective wall between commercial banks, investment banks, and other financial institutions, and it led the way to greater leveraging. The result was the creation of hybrid financial institutions with incredible leveraging power (hereafter referred to as "the banks"), the likes of which we had never seen. One devastating example is American International Group (AIG). To understand how AIG's actions caused such debilitating problems for the economy, we need to look at another unwise deregulation.

COMMODITY FUTURES MODERNIZATION ACT OF 2000

Another far-reaching legislative error was the repeal of the Shad-Johnson Jurisdictional Accord, otherwise known as *Commodity Futures Modernization Act of 2000* (CFMA). Simply, CFMA removed the regulation that required banks and other financial institutions to sell all financial products as futures contracts, which were highly regulated. This regulatory change opened the door to creatively developing new financial products to sell debt and raise capital, which led to overleveraging, which led to the rise in debt-to-asset ratios for the banks, which led to the liquidity crisis. With this regulation out of the way, financial institutions became free to do as they wished with virtually any financial instrument. Unfortunately, removing this regulation also exposed the buying and selling of financial products to what is tantamount to "a roll of the dice." AIG saw this as an opportunity to make money, and lots of it, so it rolled the dice.

AIG AND CREDIT DEFAULT SWAPS

AIG is an insurance company first, and the major financial problem on its hands now is a national problem. AIG is too big to fail because it is the largest insurer in the world. The company has 74 million outstanding insurance policies worldwide. This is something to consider when talking about "letting it fail," for sure, but something else to consider is that worldwide, many large banks and other investment institutions utilized AIG to insure many of the risky investments that are now collapsing. AIG provided the insurance utilizing the highly questionable financial instrument known as a *Credit Default Swap*[1] (CDS), which works like this: The buyer of a CDS pays a monthly premium to the seller for effectively insuring against a debt default. If the debt instrument defaults, the seller pays the agreed amount in a lump sum to the buyer of the CDS.

Because the CDS market is a large part of the economic problems we face today, illuminating this murky financial instrument helps us understand why.

JP Morgan introduced the first CDS in 1995. Within a dozen years, their total market value increased to an estimated $62 trillion, which dwarfs that of the stock market and the bond market combined, the very markets the CDS is supposed to protect. With no regulation and with so much money in play, these financial products became speculative, losing their original intent as insurance devices. Additionally, their high-trading frequency often obscures the actual owners, and their market value is so high that when a negative event occurs, the CDS providers cannot actually pay.

AIG, and others, such as the now defunct Lehman Brothers, had to pay and still have to pay out trillions on any CDS in their possession. The only way AIG can do this is with hundreds of billions in taxpayer money and the depletion of all its capital reserves. This is a big, big problem for all of us.

EXOTIC FINANCIAL PRODUCTS

With all of this "easy" money from the new subprime loans and refinanced mortgages surging into banks, cre-

---

1 "Credit Default Swaps Explained." *Economics Help,* November 11, 2008. http://www.economicshelp.org/blog/finance/credit-default-swaps-explained.

ative opportunities emerged for these same institutions to raise more capital for lending, which they needed to keep the bubble expanding. These refinance and new mortgage transactions represented cash out for *future* money, so, to re-acquire the capital dispensed in mortgages, the banks began packaging and selling the mortgages into new, exotic *Collateralized Debt Obligations*[2] (CDOs) and other mortgage-backed securities. These financial products helped spread the risk while raising capital, but creating them also began a chain of ownership that would result in cataclysmic financial losses across the globe.

SAVINGS RATE DECLINE

Another negative effect from deregulation was the lending orgy that led to the sharpest decline in the savings rate in U.S. history, resulting in a negative national savings rate. This, too, was a red flag for investors. Think about this …

Banks offer interest to attract savings so they can lend out those dollars at a higher interest rate. If a huge percentage of consumers' income is going to mortgage payments, what does that leave for the bank account, and where, then, do banks get money to lend? If more people had asked this question, things might be different today. One answer, of course, is the creation of the exotic financial products in the form of the CDOs and other mortgage-backed securities.

As lenders lent more subprime money to consumers who could not afford the houses they were buying, a percentage

---

2   Investopedia, s.v. "Collaterized Debt Obligation – CDO," http://www.investopedia.com/terms/c/cdo.asp.

of those consumers began to default on the loans. As those consumers defaulted in increasing numbers, property values began to decline. As values began to decline, high-value mortgages appeared more and more problematic, so people began selling their houses to get out from under the high debt. As more people sold, housing values declined more rapidly. Thus, the quickly moving downward spiral took off, and within two years (2005-2007), the collapse was in full swing.

The effects of the collapsing market spread like a virus into the ownership chain of CDOs and mortgage-backed securities entrenched in the global financial institutions. Quickly, this giant house of cards collapsed. Fear gripped those investors who once had cash money and now had seemingly worthless paper. That "worthless paper" had an unforeseen and extremely damaging effect on the international banking system because of new accounting rules that went into effect in the United States and Europe in November 2007, just as the foreclosure rate was spiking and real estate values were dropping off a cliff.

NEW ACCOUNTING RULES

The accounting rules change is extremely complex, and subject to much debate, which is part of the problem. So, I won't go deeply into it, nor will I endeavor to explain it in detail. It is important, though, to understand how the change in accounting rules affected the global banking system and contributed to the position we are in today.

Publicly traded companies follow a standardized set of principles for corporate accounting. These principles, the

Generally Accepted Accounting Principles (GAAP), are the basis for asset valuation. *The Federal Accounting Standard Board* (FASB), the accounting arm of the SEC, is the biggest and most powerful rules contributor to the GAAP.

Historically, loans and other financial products were put on the books at cost and not "marked" up or down unless sold or in default. After the collapse of the Savings and Loans in the late 1980s, many argued this "traditional" accounting for loans allowed banks to "hide" bad assets on their books. Thus, to rectify this perceived problem, the SEC imposed *FASB 157*[3], a new accounting methodology, on November 15, 2007. FASB 157 requires all publicly traded companies in the U.S. to classify their assets based on the certainty with which fair values can be calculated. This statement created three asset categories: Level 1, Level 2, and Level 3. Level 1 assets are the easiest to value accurately based on standard market-based prices and Level 3 assets are the most difficult.

The valuation method that fits this directive, "mark to market," was not new. It had been around for some time as a valuation method for brokers on the futures exchanges. In effect, it protected brokers. Brokers need to assess daily the value of any asset in a trader's account, in case a margin call is required. Assessing multi-trillion dollar securities with long-term value and substantial cash flow is quite different from assessing value on margin accounts. Mark-to-market valuation now put the multi-trillion dollar asset-backed

---

3   Financial Accounting Standards Board, *Summary of Statement No. 157 Fair Value Measurements,* November 15, 2007, http://www.fasb.org/st/summary/stsum157.shtml.

securities market on a valuation level equal to the daily valuations of a broker trying to keep his margined clients in line.

Mark-to-market valuation records the price or value of a security or portfolio to reflect its current market value, rather than its book value. It measures the fair value of accounts that can change over time, such as assets and liabilities. Mark to market is supposed to provide a realistic appraisal of financial institutions' current financial situation.

Ironically, in the 1980s and 1990s, scandalous corporations and banks adopted this valuation method to achieve their own greedy end, but this did not deter the SEC from imposing mark-to-market accounting for the GAAP. When the SEC proposed this accounting change prior to its adoption, plenty of smart people argued that mark-to-market accounting would exacerbate the problem that was coming into full bloom in the fall of 2007. Obviously, the high-risk, subprime assets were classified as Level 3. If the SEC had only listened to the arguments against this proposed change in the GAAP, it would have seen the effect it would have on the burgeoning credit problem.

We should assume the SEC implemented this accounting change to achieve more transparency in the seemingly flawed system, thus providing a better way to value the troubled assets. Unfortunately, in their attempt to assist with the developing valuation crisis, they only created a bigger problem. Here's why. Many firms (including some of the largest in terms of assets) had to write down billions of dollars in hard-to-value Level 3 assets following the subprime meltdown and related credit crisis, which began in late 2006. By making companies report to investors the breakdown of assets, this allowed investors to see what percentage of the balance sheet could potentially be open to revaluation or susceptible to sudden write-downs.

Layering irony on top of irony, in the attempt to fix a problem, regulators implemented a "solution" that did not consider regulations already in place. Thus, when FASB 157 (mark-to-marketing valuations) required banks to value certain financial assets on their regular financial statements based on their value as of that day, this created market volatility, understandably, but volatility was not the catalyst that propelled these toxic assets to the forefront of the financial problems. The catalyst for the most intractable problem we face in this financial crisis was the regulation that required banks to raise capital reserves to compensate for declining assets on their books. As the housing market collapsed and book valuations of financial assets dramatically dropped in value, existing regulations forced banks to raise more and more capital, which became extremely difficult in a frozen credit market. To avoid having to raise huge amounts of capital, banks tried selling the assets at extreme discounts to their future value just to get them off their books. This attracted some private capital, but not enough, as no one knew the true value of the assets.

As all valuations continued downhill and access to credit disappeared, only one entity on the planet existed that could inject the capital needed to save the entire financial system from absolute collapse, and it acted in September 2008.

At the request of the Bush administration, the U.S. Congress enacted the Troubled Assets Relief Program (TARP). This $700 billion program, designed to stop the impending collapse, worked. Although the program and its proponents received heavy criticism for how the banks utilized the money, one thing that is not disputable is that the financial system is still functioning, and it is improving as we move through this crisis.

THE RESULTS

The inevitable effects of the housing collapse and the poorly regulated banking industry was a freeze in commercial real estate lending; a freeze in bank-to-bank lending; increased credit restrictions for everyone, including the consumer, small business, and corporations; a rise in bank-to-bank lending rates, and "bad" books for most lending institutions around the world.

The pejorative and confidence-freezing phrase "toxic assets" became the buzz phrase for the vigorous and huge effort on the part of the U.S. government to "bail out" the financial sector of the economy, which led to talk of "nationalizing" the banks. Now, the word "socialism" found its way into the discussion, and this sent shivers of fear throughout the stock markets. Within weeks, they too would crash, erasing trillions of dollars in wealth in less than two months; the unemployment rate would spike to record, historical highs; the big, fat commodity bubbles (specifically oil) would burst; and the specter of deflation would rear its scary head.

Many influences contributed to the current economic problems, but contained within all of them is one essential and undeniably important ingredient: the psychology of the investor at every level. If we learn anything from studying this recession, it is this: Greed got us here and fear keeps us here.

When markets produce extraordinary returns in relatively short time periods, greed comes into play and bubbles develop. This, of course, leads to over-selling in markets, which leads to collapse. A case-in-point is the U.S. housing market, which is causing us all so much pain.

When market bubbles burst, or up turns to down in markets, confidence erodes and fear sets in. A couple of bad things can happen in these fearful conditions. We freeze up as a deer caught in the headlights of a car does, or we act like chickens chased by a fox — we run in panic. Greed takes us to the top, sends us crashing to the bottom, and fear keeps us toiling there for as long as it takes to get our confidence back.

To exemplify this, look at what happened in this country after mid-September 2008. When then Treasury Secretary Paulson announced that markets were on the verge of financial collapse, he declared that if the government did not inject huge sums of money into the top banks immediately, the system would implode. Congress acted, the capital injection occurred, and for a brief moment, stabilization set in. And then something interesting happened—or, rather, did not happen. Banks with the huge influx of capital did not resume their lending, especially to other banks. Credit dried up even further. Businesses could not get loans to meet payroll, consumers could not get credit to buy all types of consumer goods, and credit-card companies slammed the door on credit for less-than-perfect customers.

Why did this happen? Fear of what the future held is the reason. Even as the three-month London Interbank Offered Rate (LIBOR) dropped from record highs to more normal levels (above five percent to around one percent), banks still hoarded cash, and lending remained tight. A failure of confidence froze the system, and the rest is history. Frozen credit, bank failures, overall financial instability, housing price instability, a swarm of foreclosures, commodities rising to ultra-high levels, economic contraction, and rising unemployment all became signposts to a future no one wanted, or had expected six months earlier. The stock market dropped like a stone in October 2008, continued to drop through mid-November, and then bottomed. December saw a brief uptick, which lasted into early January 2009.

As detailed plans for resolving the financial crisis remained murky and the steady stream of negative economic news continued unabated, panic selling continued through February 2009, dropping the markets below the November lows and into new, dangerous territory, a place that seemed potentially bottomless.

The world owned up to the economic problems and began taking serious steps to fight the global recession in the first quarter of 2009, but by then the war was in full swing, and, in any war, fear is a natural part of the process.

All of this brings us, as investors, to an important two-part question. When are greed and fear appropriate, and when are they detrimental? To answer this question, let's take an objective look at both greed and fear in the next chapter. I will analyze how these two staples in the investment world affect us when times are good and when times are bad.

CHAPTER

— 2 —

WHAT DO WE DO?

We all would prosper more consistently if we accepted and acted upon a simple truth: Each of us has the power to change how we view the world at any given moment in time.

THE PROBLEM (FEAR AND GREED)

Clearly, these are troubled economic times. As investors, we would be wise to recognize this truth. When we do recognize this, the obvious question emerges: What do we do? The quote above sums up the foundation of what we need to do to get through these dark days. Yes, the statement is somewhat esoteric, but any successful concrete steps one would take depend on believing the implied message in the statement: In times of crisis, such as now, emotional decisions lead to failure. We all have the ability to control our emotions, and to that end, in times such as this, objectivity, clarity of purpose, and resolute action are the keys not only to surviving, but also thriving when the time is right to strike.

Before we can see our way to making money, though, we have to assess, make tough decisions, and then do our best to get through this so when the recovery comes, we have money to invest. When we do this, we must do it with objectivity, clarity of purpose, and resolute action. To do this, we must control our fear.

Are we facing the largest personal, geopolitical, and financial crisis of our lifetime? With a high degree of probability, the answer is, "Yes." Once we get out of denial and embrace the truth of what we are seeing, we are in a position to prosper. As long as we allow fear to chase after us, we are victims.

— *Dr. Janice Dorn*

Dr. Dorn, a renowned psychiatrist, teaches traders how to cope with the emotions associated with trading. Anyone who believes that emotions have little to do with trading is trading in another universe. Anyone who has traded or invested knows well the emotions of fear and greed. These emotions are not only a problem in our trading and investing, but they are a problem in everyday life for most of us. Specifically, these emotions are particularly dangerous now as we weigh our daily economic and general life choices.

MAKE GOOD CHOICES

A lesson learned about making good choices is one I learned recently when breeding cows: To get useable results, make good choices. For example, it may be cheaper to breed a purebred cow to a non-purebred bull, but it may not yield useable results. It may actually cost more money. Breeding a Holstein heifer to a non-purebred bull will produce a calf that is too large and may cause serious problems for the cow. The point is, think through your choices and make decisions based on what you know, not on the emotion of the moment.

Fundamentally, our daily choices are but two — buy or not, sell or not. These two choices resound throughout the investing community, as well as the community of everyday living. They manifest in myriad other questions whose answers have huge ramifications for us as non-investors, investors, and for the economy in general.

Should I buy a car, a new television, or go out to dinner with my family or friends? Should I pay down my debt or save for my kids' college education? Should I sell my mutual funds before it is too late? Should I dump my stock in fundamentally sound companies so I can short the financials? Should I buy gold at these peak prices? These are but a few of the questions each of us faces every day.

No one can answer the multitude of questions with any certainty. As discussed earlier, no one really knows the true extent of our problems. No one, no matter how brilliant an economist or how successful an investor, knows how or when a recession will end and the recovery will begin. What is known is that the economic downturn, no matter how bad, will end and the economy will recover. Understanding and accepting this allows you to prepare mentally and economically for that time when bad news begins morphing into good news, and the steady downhill slide turns into a gradual climb back uphill.

CHOOSING FEAR

To achieve this goal, then, it is important first to discuss in more detail the emotion of fear. A line from Dr. Dorn's earlier quote is a good place to start.

Once we get out of denial and embrace the truth of what we are seeing, we are in a position to prosper.

Hopefully, all of us have accepted that the economy, our investments, and our quality of life are threatened. The truth is no one, no matter who that person is, can offer us an easy way out. It is difficult, but keeping our wits about us, retaining our personal power of choice, and watching for the signs of recovery are our best strategy for coming through at the other end with enough resources in place to take advantage of the potential opportunities coming our way.

Refuse to operate in fear. Operating in fear is a losing proposition. This position derives from a simple understanding of markets and trading, not unfounded optimism. Markets go up and markets go down. Market crashes are part of the dynamic cycles of the markets and life. As investors, we know this, both intuitively and factually. Why, then, do we see panic and economic bloodshed on the "street"? Why is it that some investors in positions to manipulate so many are preaching such doom? To speculate is useless. Looking squarely at the problem to see where the light will eventually shine is much more useful, and I will do that shortly. For the moment, I will continue to shine the light on the danger of emotional choices in troubled times. Again, I turn to the insight of Dr. Dorn.

Survival in the markets and in life requires that we do not fall victim to the primitive fear-based rat brain, and that we move into the clear-thinking new brain. In the markets as in life, survival is not related to being the strongest or the most intelligent. Those who survive are most able to respond to change without being threatened or in denial of it.

This is the key to keeping it together. Responding to change means doing things differently. If, as a consumer, you have been running up debt on your credit card, for example, it would not be prudent to continue that behavior in this economy. If you are doing that, ask yourself the following question: Am I continuing to run up debt because I am in denial of the current economic state or, because I fear losing my job, I am trying to preserve capital?

Either way, the choice to continue doing what you are doing might not be your best choice, unless, of course, you have no choice. When choice is severely limited, you have to do what you have to do to survive. As an investor, if you have been selling your stock in fundamentally sound companies, you need to look at why you are doing that. Perhaps you need the capital, and, again, you do what you have to do. Then again, if you are selling because the media world is selling bad news and you are in fear, that is a bad choice. In fact, it might be a choice you regret when the recovery comes.

This is not a general prescription for surviving this economic downturn. Your circumstances are particularly your own, and the choices you make are particular to your needs. Just keep your wits about you and make fearless choices.

Easy to say, agreed. In reality, actualizing a lack of fear in your decision-making is more difficult. In our experience, changing mindsets is about as difficult as it gets, but that does not mean it isn't worth the effort. If we believe that this economic downturn might go on for a while, then we must also believe we need to deal with it thoughtfully to ensure both economic health and economic survival.

I have asked you to keep your wits about you and to make clear, objective, fearless choices as both an investor and as someone just looking to remain sane in this economy. Again, easy to say, so hang with me a bit more as I provide some practical insight to exactly what fear is and how you can cope with it or possibly eliminate it from your life.

According to Daniel Gardner, the author of *The Science of Fear, Why We Fear Things We Shouldn't—and Put Ourselves in Greater Danger,* irrational fear springs from how humans miscalculate risks.

Gardner expends huge amounts of language to explain why we act the way we do when fear strikes. In that large volume of words, he discusses one small idea that has particular relevance to our concerns of today: people fear big numbers in bad situations.

The example Gardner uses is the number of pedophiles prowling the Internet for our children. He cites the most commonly used authoritative number as 50,000. He argues that because authoritative figures use this number in various forms (at least 50,000, more than 50,000, or 50,000 on the nose), we tend to believe and fear it when, in actuality, no one really knows the true number. Should you fear it? No, you should not. Should you do something to protect your children against even one predator on the Internet? You bet. Here is the hard question, though: What should you do to protect your children from even one predator on the Internet? Should you tell them the Internet is no longer available to them, or would you explain to them the potential danger and then monitor their usage so you can see where they are going and what they are doing on the Internet?

The first choice is clearly an irrational, fear-based choice. The second, although not ideal, is clearly more rational. Because it is more rational, it is more likely that you will protect your children better than if you ban them from the Internet.

THINK

So how does the above example relate to us as investors and consumers? Actually, it doesn't relate directly; however, within the example is an issue of importance to us. Big numbers cause fear in bad situations. The bigger they are, the scarier they are. And when dealing with the big, bad economy, there is no shortage of big, bad numbers bandied about daily. You might hear on the news, for example, that "Corporation X announced 20,000 layoffs today," and the newscaster might follow that with "adding to the unemployment numbers which are already at the highest level on record."

This would scare anybody, no doubt, and an alarm should sound in the brain, but the rational mind should digest the information, process it, and then make a choice as how to deal with it. Yes, it is bad news, but how bad is it, really? Is it bad enough to sell off your portfolio because the Dow

Jones Industrial Average dropped 300 points the day after the news broadcast? Is it so bad that you should cancel the car you just ordered from your local dealer? The answers depend on you and your circumstances, true, but they also depend on what those "big" numbers really mean. Looking closely at those hypothetical numbers to see what they actually might mean is quite enlightening.

CONTEXTUALIZE

In an economic downturn, layoffs are common and expected. When Corporation X announces 20,000 layoffs, the first thing to do is contextualize that number. For example, what is the overall state of the economy? How far along is the recession? How many employees does the company have? How will the 20,000 layoffs affect the bottom line of that company?

Answering contextual questions just might help you make better choices. In fact, it is possible that Corporation X has 800,000 employees worldwide so 20,000 layoffs equals 2.5% of its total workforce. Although it means 20,000 join the ranks of the non-spenders, does it necessarily mean that Corporation X is in fundamentally bad shape? It could be that Corporation X, as a fundamentally sound company, is laying off deadwood in the company and that, by doing so, the bottom line will improve in six months. One might infer from this analysis that the company is okay, but the economy is getting worse.

So maybe your choice is not to sell your shares in the company, even though the stock price dropped 10% the day of the announcement. Instead, you review your whole portfolio to assess which companies are fundamentally sound and which are not. Perhaps, even though it might mean a capital loss, you decide to sell those that are not because you want to raise capital. This deliberative choice is far more practical and beneficial than selling simply because the news is bad and others are selling in fear.

As to the "unemployment numbers which are already at the highest level on record," what does this really mean? We can look at this statement in the context of the current economic problems because it is a fact that we have achieved this unemployment level for the first time in this recession.

This too is scary, and it depicts one fact that we cannot escape: The economy is in trouble. Facts are facts, right? Yes, but the issue is never just the veracity of facts. The issue is what do the facts mean to each of us? Should we fear this dramatic announcement? Absolutely not. Should we factor it into our analysis of what we do on a day-to-day basis as both an investor and a consumer? Absolutely, we should.

When the January 2009 unemployment announcement came out, panic set in. The markets sold off dramatically, resuming a bearish trend, which had been somewhat stalled since the November lows. What scared the sellers? Clearly, the unemployment numbers indicated the economic down-turn was worsening, pointing to a big concern, but what does "record level" really mean? It means more people were unemployed in December 2008 than at any other time in our history. I don't want to minimize the human suffering, but the fact is the U.S. workforce is larger than it ever has been in our history. Thus, 8% of 150 million is going to be larger than 8% of 100 million, for example. Therefore, the "record" number of unemployed, although telling about the general state of the economy, does not give us all the information we need to make rational choices.

BAD NEWS SELLS

The point is big numbers in bad situations cause fear, and the news media sells fear. In bad times, the headlines are always "big." For example, check out the following headlines.

> # Unemployment Expected To Reach 10% By Year's End
>
> # FORECLOSURES RISE TO HIGHEST LEVEL IN 30 YEARS
>
> # Seven Trillion Dollars in Stock Market Wealth Wiped Out

Again, all of this is bad news, and the media should report it, but we, as "news consumers," should consider what the news really means, and then we should act accordingly. We cannot accept it on face value and retreat to our places of fear.

Instead, if you want to understand the meaning and the reality of the employment numbers, ask some questions.

For example, how many of the newly unemployed are from the ailing financial sector? Which sector of the economy is experiencing the most layoffs? How does the technology sector compare to the service sector? Are the majority of these newly unemployed workers highly skilled or less skilled workers?

GET GOOD INFORMATION

The answers to these questions (and more) are easy and quick to find, depending on your desire and the download speed of your Internet connection. If you want facts, and only facts, regarding economic data, go to the website below, the primary source for obtaining current economic data. If you want information that will guide both your investment and consumer decisions, this is the place to start.

http://www.bls.gov

The report bypasses the media bias and goes straight to the numbers. I have included excerpts from a report, so you can get the flavor of it, as well as see how the news media uses language to sell bad news.

THE EMPLOYMENT SITUATION: FEBRUARY 2009

Nonfarm payroll employment continued to fall sharply in February (-651,000), and the unemployment rate rose from 7.6 to 8.1 percent, the Bureau of Labor Statistics of the U.S. Department of Labor reported today. Payroll employment has declined by 2.6 million in the past 4 months. In February, job losses were large and widespread across nearly all major industry sectors.

Unemployment (Household Survey Data)
Employment in financial activities continued to decline in
February (-44,000). The number of jobs has dropped by
448,000 since an employment peak in December 2006,
with half of this loss occurring in the past 6 months. In
February, job losses occurred in real estate (-11,000);
credit intermediation (-11,000); and securities, commodity
contracts, and investments (-8,000). Retail trade employ-
ment fell by 40,000 over the month and has declined by
608,000 since December 2007. In February, employ-
ment decreased in automobile dealerships (-9,000), sport-
ing goods (-9,000), furniture and home furnishing stores
(-8,000), and building material and garden supply stores
(-7,000). Employment in wholesale trade fell by 37,000
over the month, with nearly all of the decline occurring in
durable goods.

Now, compare the following sentences excerpted from the
government report with some generic headlines reporting
the same information.

- **Widespread job losses continued in manufacturing in February (–168,000).** The manufacturing
  sector shed 168,000 jobs in February, after eliminating
  257,000 positions the prior month.

- **The construction industry lost 104,000 jobs in
  February.** Construction industries bled 104,000 jobs
  in February...

- **Service industries subtracted 375,000 workers
  in February.** The service-providing industry slashed
  375,000 positions in February...

The biased language is subtle, but there. Note the words "shed," "bled," and "slashed," as well as the idea expression in sentence one. Instead of using the bland language from the report, the news media "spices" it up to get our attention and to instill a dramatic sense, which creates more fear.

This might seem irrelevant and somewhat "preachy." I understand this, but I caution that we can create our own negative, self-fulfilling prophecies if we don't take our power back by fighting fear. Fear is real and consequential, especially in troubled times.

In this era of the Internet and the 24-hour cable news cycle constantly warning of impending doom, fear is ubiquitous. Examples of how bad things are flow at us from the Internet, TV, radio, newspapers, and magazines. We get it! The economy and all of its related parts are in trouble.

DEAL WITH FEAR

Okay, accepting this naturally leads me to discuss how to deal with it. How do we conquer fear and move to a place offering hope rather than despair? How do we move from paralysis or flight to a steady place of objective thought that allows us to see the truth of where the economy is and where our place in that is? Dr. Dorn offers an answer to these questions. Although she directs that answer toward traders and investors, it nevertheless applies to all of us.

Life and the markets are not ever about what happens to us. They are about who we are, and how we respond to what happens to us. **The opposite of fear is faith,** *and I urge every one of you to have faith in yourself and your*

> *ability to navigate through and survive anything that life or the markets throws at you. Those who do this will survive to trade another day as long as clear heads prevail, stay in the moment, go with the flow and remember the lessons of history.*

It is the last line in the above quote that should bring us the most comfort, given the circumstances, and it should form the basis for our objective thought and planning for the recovery, when it comes.

THE LESSON OF HISTORY

One lesson of our history is that no matter how bad the economy gets, it will recover. Imagine how the millions of homeless, bankrupt, and poor folks in the Great Depression felt as they watched their economic world collapse around them. Imagine how the new middle class and the wealthy elite felt as their businesses went broke, their homes were repossessed, and their life savings disappeared. How must they have felt as the new medium of radio spread the word to all corners of the civilized world that "the country was going to hell in a hand basket"? How must they have felt as the political and ideological battles over how to "fix it" raged in newspapers, magazines, and on the radio?

The 1970s and the early 1980s brought more of this economic trouble and its associated fear. With the technological progress of the media, we had more bad news more often. Television, syndicated radio, movies, newspapers, and magazines constantly gave us all more examples of the bad economy. Think about how you felt if you were there. In fact, think about how you feel right now, today, suffering under the constant bombardment of bad news.

Here is the lesson, again. For all the doom and gloom in our historically dire and economically horrible situations, the economy came back stronger and with more opportunity for everyone. History will repeat itself here, and the economy will come back stronger and with more opportunity. As always, though, the question is when.

The answer is unknown, but that should not stop us from fighting fear and fighting to regain our economic status where and when we can. In fact, it is imperative that we do so. Aside from the obvious troubles in the housing, financial, credit, and labor markets, one could plausibly argue that the single most critical factor in any recovery is the consumer. In short, all of us, together and individually, can help solve our problems.

Economic forecasts predict up to a $1.5 trillion decline in consumer spending for 2009. This is a huge hit to a $14 trillion economy dependent on consumer spending to the tune of 72%. Yes, much of this spending deficit derives from real people in real economic trouble, and there is little these folks can do to fight back, but we must not forget that 90% of us are not in fatal trouble. To varying degrees, we all face economic issues, and some of us are on the verge of real trouble, which makes our responsibility to fight back even greater. I propose a different perspective on our problems is the best way to fight back.

A DIFFERENT PERSPECTIVE

The savings rate in America has for too long been negative. Ironically, last year, the savings rate went from a negative to one of the highest positive rates in decades. In February, the savings rate went above 5%. In the overall scheme, this is both prudent and good for the economy. High savings rates mean banks have more money to lend, which can only help the economy. Saving money and reducing spending is a rational choice to protect against the potential of darker economic days. At the same time, the motivation for the savings rate increase and decrease in spending is fear-based. With all of the bad news, no one knows what tomorrow will bring. Okay. How about this, though?

We should adopt the attitude that we will return to a more normal life as financial prudence permits. We should clearly see the economy as one in trouble, to be sure, but also as one that will recover. When we see encouraging signs of potential recovery, we should then take small steps toward a more normal life. We should all commit to doing one thing that we stopped doing when all this bad economic stuff started raining down upon us. Here are some possible scenarios.

If you make a solid family income, your debt is low, your savings are high, and you know your jobs are safe, then maybe you could buy that car you desperately needed back in October 2008. You might even buy an American car from one of the more financially sound carmakers. If not, buying a foreign car helps as well. If not a car, then maybe buying that new HDTV your kids have been asking for or taking a mini vacation as a family might soften the hard edge of fear.

If your family income is not huge but your debt is low, your savings are high, and you know your jobs are safe, go out for that regular family dinner you gave up when this economic tempest rushed in. Go out to a local restaurant and relax. Dining out with family might relieve some of the anxiety that hangs in the air these days, and it helps the local economy, which we all know is the footing of the national economy.

If you have a little money, are working, and your debt is low, reach out to the less fortunate in your community. Donate five dollars to those who are on the front line of taking care of the less fortunate. In fact, this is good for all of us to do in these trying times. Remember, what goes around, comes around.

TRADERPLANET.COM

At TraderPlanet.com, we practice this philosophy daily. It is in our highest and best interest to give back part of what we make as investors and traders. To become better at what we do, we need to raise our consciousness to include an awareness of our surroundings, whether it is watching the flow of dollars in a new economy or seeing others who are less fortunate.

TraderPlanet® encourages its members to use some of their trading profits for good. To achieve this objective, we've established The TraderPlanet Charity of the Month, a poll which encourages members to donate to the featured charities, recommend and vote on those for consideration, and ultimately decide the most productive way to apply these proceeds. TraderPlanet supports charities that champion health, environmental, human rights and animal welfare issues. The TraderPlanet community donated nearly $70,000 in grants in the first four months after being launched in January 2009.

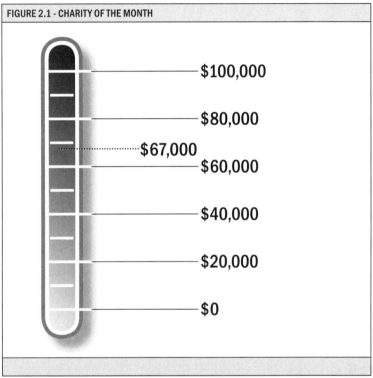

FIGURE 2.1 - CHARITY OF THE MONTH

$100,000

$80,000

$67,000

$60,000

$40,000

$20,000

$0

SOURCE: TRADERPLANET.COM.

If financial prudence allows, and we all commit to doing one thing we stopped doing when the economy turned sharply downhill, then that is the psychological beginning of the recovery. This simple act on a large scale will refuel the engine that drives the economy, and it will begin the process of healing many of the economic ills that plague us now. Perhaps one more quote from Dr. Dorn will solidify the point.

Now is the time for the true survivors to show themselves. Of all the tools in the trading and living toolbox, the most critical for survival are character, personality, thinking style, and worldview.

Ultimately, our economic survival and, by extension, U.S. survival as a strong and prosperous economy (as one part of a global economy) depends on us. We can choose to act differently all the time by fighting fear. We can choose to contribute positively to the economic recovery once we conquer fear, objectively assess our individual financial situation, and then act differently if financial prudence allows. As consumers, we can do this. As Americans and citizens of the world, we need to do this.

THE CONUNDRUM

Investors are consumers as well, so all of what I just discussed also applies to investors; however, investors frame the economic troubles somewhat differently. Because of this separate but equal viewpoint, investors operate more deeply within the economy itself. We see things that can easily generate a higher fear level about the future. In fact, assessing the economic future is the engine that drives the stock market. If our assessment is fearful, that potential future becomes our negative present. If we assess the potential future as hopeful, then our present is positive. This is quite the conundrum, true, but a solution lies within the seeming paradox.

THE SOLUTION (GREED AND FEAR)

In the late 1990s, the technological boom was creating new horizons that seemed limitless. Alan Greenspan, then Federal Reserve Chairman and one of the strongest supporters for repealing Glass-Steagall, described the resulting market bubble as "irrational exuberance." This prescient phrase pointed to the eventual collapse of the high-tech bubble, but, remember, that bubble began somewhere as a seed.

We call that seed greed, and when it sprouts, it flourishes like a weed. At first, the lush covering pleasantly seduces us to its rich and luxurious feel. We like the wide, green mat it forms as it begins to cover all that was brown and void. We like it and revel in it, to the point that we fail to see that the beautiful green has spread its tendrils, reaching in, tangling about, and eventually strangling off the life flow of the energy that gave birth to it. This is greed, but within its destructive power is the solution to the aforementioned conundrum.

When I wrote my "weed-picking" analogy in the Preface of this book, I was thinking about the overall analogy of something wonderful (seed=investment) turning into something terrible (weed=greed). One lesson my mother taught me that day was that, to get rid of the weed, you have to root it all out. Be careful, though. Don't "over pull." Remember—and this is important— a weed is only an undesired plant gaining ground at the expense of other plants. If it is not a weed, it is a desired plant.

In the movie Wall Street, Gordon Gekko claims that "greed is good." As the story moves along, however, we see the corrupting influence of greed and, as is reasonable, we conclude that greed is not good; it is bad. Unfortunately, those who follow greed to eventual destruction support this notion, and so our opinion of greed is, well, negative. Like fear, though, greed can be a positive catalyst as well as a destructive force. In fact, neither greed nor fear is the problem unto itself; rather, it is how we humans deal with these emotions that causes the problems or enhances the opportunities.

Fear is good if a man with a big gun is chasing you and you run fast to get away. Fear is bad if you freeze up when the man with a big gun is chasing you. By the same measure, greed is good if an opportunity presents itself and you prudently maximize your return on your investment in that opportunity. Greed is bad if you overextend your resources to achieve an unreasonable return on your investment in that opportunity.

Accepting this notion that greed and fear are not necessarily bad reveals the solution to the conundrum of creating a self-fulfilling prophecy regarding the potential future. If we see a negative potential future, we should not fear it, as it may or may not come to pass. Instead, with a wary mind and cautious moves, we should embrace the negative potential future as a potential investment opportunity, which is the essence of greed—identifying good investment opportunities and wisely acting on them. As Warren Buffet has simply, yet elegantly stated, "When other investors are greedy, be fearful. When other investors are fearful, be greedy."

I don't take this literally, as you now know my position on greed and fear, but I do get the message. Opportunity exists in fearful environments and potential loss of investment exists in greedy environments.

Some call this philosophy "contrarian." I agree with the title. In fact, I would argue that a contrarian investment/trading philosophy is a sure-fire way to be successful. All you need is a motivated seller, a willingness to negotiate to your bottom line, a willing buyer, and a certain amount of due diligence.

For example, in the current economy, many have pulled back from buying. Selling is their way to deal with whatever fear or needs they may have. Recently, I applied my contrarian philosophy in one of my favorite investment endeavors, raising and selling animals. Knowing the current environment favors buyers, I searched out a woman selling 16 sheep. Clearly, for whatever reason, she had a need to sell the sheep at less than market value. I bought them from her at my bottom-line price and then sold them all within 24 hours, making a tidy profit. Creating a market (no matter how big or small) in tough economic times is one way to make the seed of greed work for you without harming yourself or others.

PERCEPTION IS REALITY

In this horribly fearful environment today, investors see a negative potential future, and so they sell in fear. Consequently, the downward spiral accelerates because, as investors sell in fear, the markets go down. As the markets go down, overall confidence in the economy erodes. Fearful consumers pull back from their normal lifestyles and demand slows. As businesses feel that slack, they too begin to pull back. Reinvestment dollars dry up, production slows, layoffs occur, and the ensuing whirlpool of negativity swallows us all.

I understand that this market "psychology" is huge, and the fact of the matter is that our suggestion that we all operate differently in this negative cycle will not change the overall flow toward the bottom. Because the mass investor-consciousness still operates in the negative realms of fear and greed, we all suffer. This does not mean, however, that as individuals each of us cannot change our own investor consciousness to better our own position. Again, referencing the single most successful investor of our time, Warren Buffet, if he possesses this mindset and he successfully invests within this framework, why aren't each of us doing the same? Isn't success our goal? Don't we want to succeed?

WHAT DOES THIS MEAN TO US?

Practically, then, what does this psychological concept mean to us in this current negative environment? The answer exists in four parts.

PART 1

Without a doubt, the most important part is to accept that whatever we are experiencing now will pass, and the markets will return to a positive state. History has proven this, as the DJIA chart for the last 109 years clearly shows. Not only have the markets returned healthy and prosperous after every downturn, but also the prevailing and unstoppable trend is up.

Two things in the chart will help us understand the psychological importance of "perception is reality." First, in

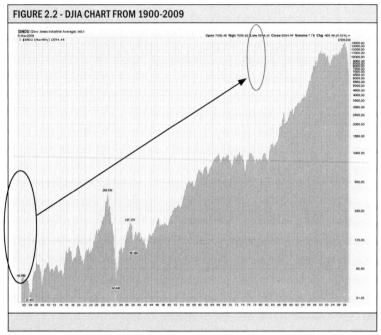

the worst of all DJIA drops (1929-1933), the market recovered. Second, the current downturn hardly compares as a percentage to the worst of all DJIA downturns. True, more wealth has been displaced in this downturn, but that is because more wealth is involved. The point is that to come back from this downturn will take a lot less time than the one in 1929-1933—assuming, of course, that the collapse is just about done. Remember, the issue is not "if" we recover, the issue is "when."

Without accepting this fundamental truth, we cannot move past this point. Our vision of a negative potential future is the reason for the negative present in the stock market.

Despite those talking heads, analysts, and pundits who keep reminding us of our bleak future—we are headed toward a depression, the DJIA could hit 3500, the financial/housing crisis persists, our adding to the debt will cause terrible future inflation—we know better. Our future in the stock market is what our mass consciousness makes it. All those many things might happen, or they might not, but if we believe they will, then our negative present is very, very real. Here is our suggestion.

Accept the possibility that the near-to-mid-term economic outlook for 2009 into 2010 is weak with deepening problems in the short term. Accept that the stock market will continue in a negative or volatile pattern during that near-to-mid-term future while it continues to search for a bottom.

Okay. Have you accepted these two things? Now, embrace the historical fact that the economy and the stock market will recover. If you do this, your investor brain should then focus on a hopeful future, which will create a positive present. Now, this positive present will still have all of the economic and market problems occurring in real time, but fear won't muddy your thinking. Accept the reality that we have serious problems and will have them for some time. Accept the reality that the economy and the markets will recover. Accept Dr. Dorn's words.

Since the inception of trade, there have been manias, panics, and crashes. They are part of the ever-changing cycles of the markets and life.

A Brief Timeline for Historical Manias and Bubbles

- Tulip Mania (1637)
- The South Sea Company (1720)
- Mississippi Company (1720)
- Railway Mania (1840s)
- Florida Speculative Building (1926)
- 1920s American Economy (1922-1929)
- The Nifty Fifty American Stocks (1960s, early 1970s)
- Japanese Asset Prices (1980s)
- The Dot-com Mania (1995–2001)
- 1997 Asian Financial Crisis (1997)
- Oil Spike (2008)
- Global Real Estate (current)
- Global Financial Crisis (current)

PART 2

The second part of the answer to the question, what does this mean to us in the current negative environment is: Define your resource availability. If you have removed the fear from your thinking, you can then start realistically analyzing your available resources. This practical element is critical because in this volatile and fluid market environment, one has to be extremely careful with precious resources. The goal is to make future dollars, not lose present dollars, remembering the fundamental investment rule: Preserve and protect capital even above making money.

Ask yourself, first and foremost, do I want to risk any capital at all in these markets? If you do not, this does not mean you do nothing; quite the opposite, in fact. Pay close attention to the everyday happenings in the markets. Listen to all reputable economic, financial, and stock market thinkers. Don't latch onto just one. Absorb the information and critically evaluate it. Separate the wheat from the chaff and then blend all the information into your own perspective. Learn whatever you can about the areas you want to invest in when the time is right. Be a sponge and get better at what you do.

PART 3

The third part of the overall answer is to define your risk appetite. If you believe the future is positive, based on solid analysis, then define how much capital you can lose without hurting yourself, if your assumptions turn out to be incorrect. One way to go about this is to define a small amount of capital to test the waters. Find the absolute strongest candidates in the strongest sectors and lay down some low dollars. Watch your investments. If they slide, set stops or let them go. If they move up in a solid trend, begin to buy up more without breaking out of your defined risk limits. Taking this route both augments part two above and allows you to "get the feel of your investments" and gives you a sense of the investing climate.

PART 4

The fourth and final part is to develop and implement a plan. That plan should be as detailed as you can make it. It should contain specific data points to watch for continued positive movement. These data points, or signs, should act as leading indicators for your investing approach. Add to your plan potential breakout sectors and the reasons why you believe those sectors will be strong. If you do this, you will find your data points for those sectors. Do the same for the specific investment areas where you invest, whether it is forex, stocks, commodities, or futures. Define your entry and exit strategies, including dollars allocated, percentage stops, and profit targets. Be resolute and disciplined.

The recovery will come, no doubt, but when, no one knows. We can be certain that it will be a gradual and bumpy turn to the positive, however. In this bumpy ride is investment opportunity. Once we all feel the bottom beneath us, we will test that bottom until it holds. Once confidence returns to the market, more and more investors will begin testing the rising waters with defined-risk capital. A little in, a little out will be the approach until the markets show overall stability and a definitive lack of fear. Reasonable volatility provides excellent opportunities for day trading, guerilla trading, swing trading, and buy-on-the-upside building of a long-term portfolio.

This is all quite a mouthful to chew, but make the effort. The bad and slanted news that comes at us hard every day is disheartening, but so are natural disasters. We always manage to recover from natural disasters, and we will recover from where we are now, which begs the question, "Where, exactly, are we?"

CHAPTER
— 3 —

WHERE, EXACTLY, ARE WE?

Where we are today is, to a large degree, a result of political and economic decisions made in 1999, as stated earlier; however, the philosophical background of how we arrived at those fateful decisions made in 1999 is enlightening and helpful to understanding how we got here, where we are, and where we might go in the future.

THE BACK-STORY

The back-story begins with the philosophical thoughts of an eccentric and somewhat absent-minded man living in liberal thinking and revolutionary times. In 1776, Adam Smith wrote a treatise titled, *An Inquiry into the Nature and Causes of the Wealth of Nations.* This book is widely regarded as the first thoroughly developed philosophy advocating a free-market economy as more productive and more beneficial to society. Concurrent with the advent of the Industrial Revolution, this philosophy set the stage for the rapid development and expansion of the Industrial Revolution, primarily because governments and industrialists saw capitalism as the ticket to extreme wealth. This viewpoint, derived from the fundamental element of capitalism, espoused that, if left alone, with no government regulation or interference, unfettered capitalism (*laissez-faire*) would produce a rising tide that would lift all boats. If let unfettered, capitalism would produce the greatest amount of benefit for society.

UNFETTERED CAPITALISM

Certainly, for most of the 19th century, laissez-faire capitalism provided the engine for the Industrial Revolution, a time of phenomenal technological and industrial development and the beginnings of a strong middle class in America. But, with this upsurge in wealth, there also came a rise in poverty in the cities, a downturn in the quality of life for urban dwellers, and a general exploitation of workers everywhere. The rapid growth and rise in wealth for the upper classes evolved into what has been called the age of the robber barons, and the overriding public perception turned to the idea that these capitalists would do anything, sacrifice anyone, to pursue wealth. In this environment, the battle lines were drawn.

It took a while, but late in the 19th century, government finally began to intervene with such regulations as defined workdays, child labor laws, and minimal health and safety standards. The government also attacked the power of robber-baron monopolies with regulation, such as the Sherman Anti-Trust Act of 1890, which spoke to the power of large corporations wielding undue influence on the political structure and exerting too much control over supply and demand elements of capitalism. Budding labor unions joined the fight against unregulated capitalism.

With government intervention to regulate capitalism in ways unknown, the philosophical debate blossomed. The question of whether laissez-faire capitalism was good or evil formed the context and the basis of political and economic arguments then and it still does today. For example, Alan Greenspan, former Chairman of the Federal Reserve, once wrote that the Sherman Anti-Trust Act of 1898 killed off massive potential for new products, processes, machines, and cost-saving mergers before they could be born. He further suggested that the act kept our standard of living lower than it might have been otherwise been.

People in political power and positions of influence made such arguments in the post-war 1920s, an era of freewheeling deregulation that resulted in the wild times we historically refer to as "The Roaring Twenties." That era of deregulation and low taxes gave such a strong shot to the economy that the wealthy elite and the middle class enjoyed quite a nice rise in wealth and prosperity. Times were so good that many believed the "good times are here to stay," which led to excesses in all quarters. This is eerily similar to what we experienced earlier in this decade when we did experience a rapid rise in prosperity and wealth in most all economic areas from late 2003 until mid-2007. The stock market went higher than ever, more people owned homes than ever before, and job creation went from negative to positive. Life seemed pretty darn good, didn't it?

Again, similar to the 1920s, those good times came to a crashing halt because those in power believed that the forces of capitalism and competition would determine appropriate levels of supply and demand, that those with money and power would never violate the fundamental tenet of investing: Protect and preserve capital even beyond making money.

Referring to the role he played in deregulating the banking system, a congressional representative asked Alan Greenspan, "What do you think you did wrong?" Greenspan responded, essentially, "I believed the banks would regulate themselves." Clearly, they did not. Those decision makers in the banking system let greed drive them to the point of self-destruction, which has resulted in the consequences we are experiencing today.

UNREGULATED CAPITALISM: HAS IT WORKED?

Historically, capitalists and consumers who succumbed to the allure of greed in a freewheeling, prosperous environment brought about with deregulation and low taxes created a dangerous economic environment. Today, banks, homeowners, consumers, investment institutions, and investors in general overleveraged, which has led to crashes in all markets.

After the 1920s, the Great Depression led to a highly regulated economy that fundamentally went unchallenged until the early 1970s. From about 1950, or so, until the early 1970s, America experienced the single greatest expansion of its middle class and the longest running period of wealth creation in its history. With the recession of the early 1970s, this prosperity appeared to be ending, and the philosophical battle resumed. Lower taxes and deregulation came to the fore, and, once again, the recession ended, at least temporarily.

By the end of the 1970s, the economy was once again in shambles, and the incoming administration in 1980 inherited a horrible economic mess. The solution that was offered included lower taxes and deregulation, but this time the proponents of this philosophy added a new element to the mix by increasing government spending, especially on national defense. It seemed deficits no longer mattered, and the 1980s produced another pattern of creating rapid wealth that generates market bubbles. The good times, once again, were here to stay, or so we thought.

By the middle of the 1980s, home ownership hit an all-time high, real estate values rose to an all-time high, banks (savings and loans, primarily) were lending at a record rate, and the American consumer was taking on debt and living in record prosperity. Junk bonds were the darling of Wall Street.

Once more, the seemingly inevitable happened: The IOUs came due. In 1987, the stock market crashed (Black Monday), the deregulated and overleveraged savings and loans finished collapsing in 1989, the real estate market contracted until 1995, foreclosures rose, and the party ended with another recession and a huge national debt. This recession had enough global reach to collapse the powerful Japanese economy because so many Japanese investors and banks overleveraged themselves on a global scale, with enough of that overreach invested in the U.S. and Japanese real estate markets.

This juncture in history is important to understand as it relates to the philosophical issues of unfettered capitalism, but it also points to an example that the seed of greed is a good thing to nourish and a bad thing when it gets out of control.

About this time, my dad, Louis Mendelsohn, who had been developing the idea of intermarket analysis, noted how the huge losses of the Japanese investors simultaneously sent ripples through both the Japanese and U.S. markets as the real estate market broke down. Clearly, greed got the best of the investors who were pouring money into over-heated U.S. and Japanese real estate markets in the late 1980s.

Building upon his achievements as a pioneer in technical analysis software, my dad recognized early on that the emerging globalization of the world's financial markets would permanently alter the scope of technical analysis and its application to the financial markets.

Looking at it from another viewpoint, he saw this as an opportunity to take trading software to the next level. He understood that single-market analysis (analyzing markets in isolation) no longer worked, and the Japanese economic collapse demonstrated this. So, he put his money and time into refining his idea that in a time where information is moving faster and further around the globe, all markets influence one another (intermarket analysis) to some degree. It would take him until 1991 to release the first version of VantagePoint, the predictive software based on intermarket analysis and neural networks, but, in those lean years, it is clear that he took the seed of his idea and nourished it. It is clear that this is an example of what good can come from planting the seed of greed and not letting it get out of control.

The early 1990s felt the brunt of the 1980s overindulgence, but this time something changed as politicians figured out something. The tax-cut, raise-the-deficit approach did not solve the problem of boom-and-bust cycles.

In the mid 1990s, a Republican congress and a Democratic president actually worked together to formulate a blend of philosophy that created 22 million new jobs, drove real wages up, increased corporate profits, drove the stock market up (into a tech bubble, unfortunately), raised real estate values, and, once again, expanded the middle class. In fact, in 1993, the government actually raised taxes and cut spending, which many would argue was the reason for the economic expansion. Be that as it may, one thing that is not arguable is that the tax structure and the spending controls actually eliminated the U.S. federal deficit and produced a budget surplus two years running (1999-2000) and the five-year budget projection in the year 2000 pointed to an elimination of the nation's debt. As well, it produced a projected multi-trillion dollar surplus, which could have been used to repair the healthcare system and problems with entitlement programs such as Social Security and Medicare.

All of that promise disappeared in 1999 when Congress, forgetting what it had just accomplished, passed legislation repealing the Bank Act of 1933. Remember, Congress enacted that legislation in 1933 to prevent the very thing that has just happened to the banking system today.

Once again, the philosophy that unfettered capitalism is the tide that raises all boats roared back into the political discourse, but this time we compounded the coming problems because we also forgot what we had learned about tax cuts in conjunction with rising government spending. The potential surplus envisioned five years out in 2000 evaporated with the huge tax cuts implemented in 2001 and 2003 (on top of fighting two wars) and a Congress that spent money without constraint. The President did not veto a single spending bill from 2001 to 2006.

This money, along with all of the money flowing into the markets from tax cuts (especially into real estate) and banks overleveraging heated up the markets, producing a euphoria that addicts will tell you is what drives their every move—more is better. As the party rolled on, consumer, financial, and national debt just kept on climbing, the bubbles just kept inflating, and we all acted as if this is just how it should be. Why couldn't we have it all? Just charge up the card, apply for a loan, make a loan, or invest in any market, at any time. In all cases, the easy money flowed …

Once again, the predictable result occurred. Excessive greed drove the economic engine really fast. And here we are today in a twisted heap with the banking system in virtual collapse, the stock market reeling, the housing market collapsed, consumer spending at record lows, unemployment at record highs, corporate profits disappearing, higher government spending, rising deficits, rising debt, and all-around confidence shattered.

It is clear to see the economic, philosophical battles that have shaped the political policies in the last few hundred years. It is also clear that unfettered capitalism produces boom-and-bust cycles that are extreme in both the power to build wealth and the power to destroy wealth.

Understand, I take no position as to right or wrong in the debate regarding the philosophical economic argument. My job is to lay out the facts so you can see and clearly understand how we arrived here. My goal in this is to present a mindset that allows you to make more informed investment choices now and in the future. We all need to recognize early signs of bubbles building and to take considered measures to protect assets against the inevitable collapse of those bubbles. We all need to reject the abuses inherent in an economic system that encourages excess in all of its forms.

TODAY'S REALITY

Illuminating the political/philosophical back-story of how we arrived at this place provides a much-needed context to both frame the wide debate and to help us understand our own investment philosophy. Understanding what the argument is about and analyzing the facts regarding the overall political/philosophical context gives us an important investment tool—objectivity. You see, if we put aside our biases and deal with just the facts in our analyses, we can better assess where we are and how we will get out of the mess we have on our hands today. We will see the investment environment more clearly, which improves our edge, increasing the likelihood of investment success.

Explaining how we got here raises our investment consciousness, hopefully. If we raise our investment consciousness, we will all become more aware, and we will recognize any future signs of impending collapse in any or all of the markets. We will also know what identifies a sure sign of impending recovery. Looking squarely at the problems we face, however, is the only way we will ever make fearless, objective, and clear-minded decisions regarding our potential investments.

I have already provided much information about the economic problems we face today, and I suspect you are well aware of those problems as well. However, I feel it is important in this discussion to focus tightly on the essence of the problems we have, and to provide an objective frame to view them. This frame will help illuminate the reality behind the problems.

ECONOMIC PROBLEMS

The problems we face are numerous and powerful, but, essentially, they all derive from a set of larger problems that have come together in such a way that no other economic downturn in history fully compares. This perfect storm of colliding economic events is difficult to gauge in its entirety, other than to conclude that we are in trouble, so we will look at each of the problems individually in an order that demonstrates the "chain reaction" effect the problems have on each other and the synergistic power that chain reactions produce.

Ethics and Morality

Without a doubt, a lack of ethics and a dysfunctional moral compass are at the top of the list of reasons for the state of affairs today. The CEOs who made greed-based decisions, politicians who implemented flawed deregulation policy, criminal investors who stole billions with fraudulent schemes, soulless traders who manipulated markets, and consumers who leveraged themselves to buy more than they could afford in just about every category demonstrated a serious ethical lapse. In some cases, their behavior even demonstrated a lack of moral awareness.

The choices made created this economic debacle. A lack of ethics and morals formed a wide foundation for the house of cards that has collapsed around us. Without that foundation, none of this could have happened. Until we find a way to instill a strong sense of ethics and moral behavior into our future business leaders, politicians, and market participants, we will keep inflating bubbles only to see them burst.

Real Estate Bubble

Bubbles often usher in an economic downturn, but rarely does one catalyze a worldwide recession of such magnitude. The real estate bubble pushed residential and commercial property prices beyond rationality, but even as prices soared to astronomical levels, buyers kept coming into the market.

Normally, this buying pressure is relieved when prices reach a level that begins to close the door of affordability for many potential buyers. Simply, buyers price out of the

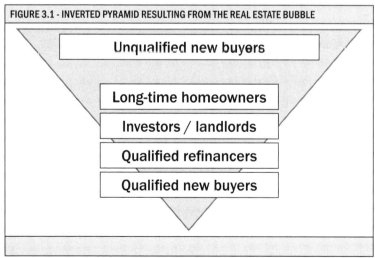

FIGURE 3.1 - INVERTED PYRAMID RESULTING FROM THE REAL ESTATE BUBBLE

Unqualified new buyers

Long-time homeowners

Investors / landlords

Qualified refinancers

Qualified new buyers

market because they cannot qualify for a loan. This did not happen in this bubble. In fact, the opposite occurred, which turned the whole process into an inverted pyramid. The unqualified buyers at the top of the upside-down pyramid became the crushing weight that crashed the system. These people would become the source of the record rise in the foreclosure rate and the source of the toxic assets that ignited the near collapse of the financial system. The speculators who added fuel to the heated upsurge in prices also brought down some heavy weight upon those who acted within the ethical and practical parameters of real estate investment.

The folks in the next four rungs, particularly those in the bottom two rungs, suffered heavily in the collapse, and they are one key contributive element to the economic recession. As these folks bought or refinanced near the top of the market in late 2006 and early 2007, taking out mortgages that did not reflect the soon-to-be true value of the property they were borrowing against, they found themselves "upside down" or on their way to it. This means the money owed to a lender is greater than the value of the property. They found themselves in this position because property values began an unprecedented rapid, double-digit percentage fall just after the last market peak.

Values dropped quickly in direct relation to the accelerating rise in foreclosures in 2007. The number of U.S. homes that slipped into foreclosure in 2007 was 79 percent higher than the previous year. The rapid rise in foreclosures and the ensuing rapid decline in property values ignited the banking liquidity crisis, which created the credit crunch. By mid-September 2008, the relationship between these factors and

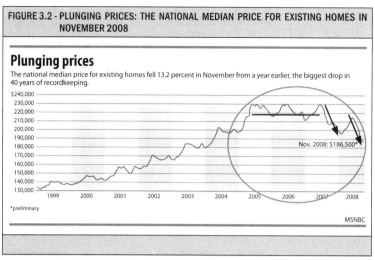

FIGURE 3.2 - PLUNGING PRICES: THE NATIONAL MEDIAN PRICE FOR EXISTING HOMES IN NOVEMBER 2008

Plunging prices

The national median price for existing homes fell 13.2 percent in November from a year earlier, the biggest drop in 40 years of recordkeeping.

Nov. 2008: $186,500*

*preliminary

MSNBC

SOURCE: NATIONAL ASSOCIATION OF REALTORS

the banks holding enormous amounts of toxic assets clarified sharply, and the economic world stumbled to its knees.

The liquidity and credit crisis that emerged from the housing market collapse shocked the economy in late September 2008, but the fact is the nation was already in recession and had been for nine months, as revealed by official statistics in hindsight.

One strong contributor to the recessionary slide was that the middle-class status of the people in the bottom four rungs comprised a large percentage of the discretionary spending in the economy. Consequently, when they found themselves upside down in their properties, they immediately shut down unnecessary spending. The long-time homeowners witnessed a dramatic drop in their net worth, which rocked their stability. Investors and landlords experienced the same drop in asset value and net worth, as well as a cessation of their reliable credit lines for potential new purchases or needed reparations. As immediate and contributive as this was to the recession, the much larger contribution came from those qualified income earners in late 2007 who had to refinance their property to get out of a potentially disastrous monthly payment increase when their adjustable rate mortgage monthly payment went up.

Freddie Mac announced that in the fourth quarter of 2007, 92 percent of prime borrowers who originally had a 1-year conforming adjustable rate mortgage (ARM) chose a new conforming fixed-rate mortgage when they refinanced and 89 percent of prime borrowers who initially had a conforming hybrid ARM refinanced into a conforming fixed-rate loan as well.

Along with the refinancers, those qualified income-earners who had just paid out sums of cash to buy their property found themselves not only upside down but with the sickening realization that they had just entered into a bad financial transaction. Psychologically, this "bad transaction" mindset sent shock waves through the economy. The immediate impact appeared as a drop in consumer spending, which accelerated the downward slide, moving the economy deeper into recession.

The above problem directly sprouts from the primary reason we are in this mess—a lack of ethics among so many and a dysfunctional moral compass for a powerful few. This connection was the first in a domino-like chain of events that brought the economy to its knees. The next domino to fall in this cascade of collapse was bank liquidity, which almost simultaneously knocked out credit for banks, corporations, small businesses, consumers, and economically hard-hit states right here in these United States.

Liquidity Crisis

Liquidity is a dry financial term, hardly interesting to anyone other than those who deal with financial issues, such as economists and bankers. As investors, though, we should not only be familiar with the term, but we should embrace it as part of our investment vocabulary. When we understand its essential meaning, the word speaks volumes about everything from the soundness of an investment to the state of the economy.

Fundamentally, liquidity means how much cash you have or can get quickly from selling assets. Cash in your wallet is liquid. Secured assets are liquid, if the market for them exists and is active, which is the rub. In September 2008, when Secretary Paulson revealed the dire nature of the banking crisis, the commercial market for secured assets had dried up like a small puddle on a hot day.

Secured assets that banks and their creditors believed were liquid suddenly became illiquid. There were two big reasons for this. Number one, the exotic CDO market that emerged when banks needed to raise capital to fuel the housing bubble essentially dried up. Thus, banks found themselves with lots of debt and nowhere to sell it. In conjunction with mark-to-market accounting and regulatory requirements, banks then needed to raise their levels of capital reserves to cover the increasing debt appearing on their regular financial statements.

In short, banks began running out of cash, and a substantial percentage of their secured assets had little to no value because an active market for selling them no longer existed. In fact, those investors and financial institutions in the U.S. and around the globe who bought trillions of dollars of exotic CDOs, as well as other, more standard, derivatives faced the possibility of holding nothing but worthless paper.

This incredibly difficult and intractable problem would soon become the central focus in the economic war because of its inherent paradox—the secured assets had no value because no market for them existed, and no market existed for the assets because they had no value. The conundrum froze every possible solution to the problem because, to create a private-capital market to buy and sell the assets, banks had to have a way to value them. The question on the lips of everyone charged with solving this horrendous problem became: How do we value these assets? This is the reason for the pejorative and confidence-crushing name, *toxic assets.*

Another ironic twist in this liquidity crisis is that some of the financial institutions hit the hardest are those that crossed the line between investment and commercial banking after the repeal of Glass–Steagall. One prime example is Citigroup, a commercial bank that morphed into a hybrid investment bank. Like AIG, it too was deemed "too big to fail." Combined, AIG and Citigroup have taken approximately $225 billion from the Federal Reserve to recapitalize, which saved them from failure, as both suffered in the broken secured-asset, commercial paper market (mortgages and packaged CDOs). Mark-to-market accounting and the collapsed housing market made the assets, at least on paper, virtually worthless. This debilitating reality spread like an oil spill on water into the overall commercial paper market and, as it did, another domino fell.

Business Credit Crunch

The commercial paper market is the second big reason for the liquidity crisis—specifically, the secured assets market, but, as we have seen, the dominoes keep falling, one hitting another, on and on. The liquidity crisis knocked the economy right into the next big problem—the commercial paper market freeze, which created the business credit crunch.

Commercial paper is short-term debt that big businesses and financial institutions sell primarily to money market funds and other institutional investors. This market raises capital for loans that companies use to fund day-to-day business operations. The simultaneous commercial paper market freeze and the drying up of the CDO and derivatives market had the same effect on the economy as a 100-pound boulder dropped into a pond from 20 feet high. At first, tremendous displacement occurs, and then ripples roll out forcefully in concentric circles. Here are some numbers from October 2008 that demonstrate the force of these two problems coming together.

Total commercial paper outstanding shrunk by $61.5 billion, or 4.1%, to a seasonally adjusted $1.45 trillion in the week ended Oct. 22, according to the latest figures from the Federal Reserve.... The latest weekly contraction marks the second-biggest percentage drop during the recent slide, and is much greater than the 2.6% decline in the previous week.[1]

---

1   http://money.ccn.com, October 23, 2008.

The $1.45 trillion number represents a half-trillion-dollar drop from the previous year, but that was not the worst of it. The rapid and continuing decline in the commercial paper market is what brought all of this into confluence.

Commercial paper outstanding, which is now at its lowest point since April 2005, has been steadily declining since Lehman Brothers' bankruptcy filing on Sept. 15. In fact, since then, total commercial paper has plunged by 20.2%—the greatest drop on record.[2]

The effect of this drop in availability of commercial paper had a profound impact on bank liquidity and business credit throughout the world. Loans, even for the biggest of the big global corporations, were no longer available.

The ripple effect pushed Europe and Asia deeper into recession immediately. As bad as this was, it was not the worst of it for the U.S. market. The powerful ripple effect sent the economy into a tailspin. If businesses cannot get money to pay ongoing bills, such as payroll, what are they going to do?

Consumer Credit Crunch

The answer, of course, is lay off workers, and this is precisely what started to happen in a big, big way in December, January, February, March, and April, when the number of newly and continually unemployed workers rose to historical highs, causing a sharp spike in the unemployment rate. Rising unemployment and upside-down property owners contributed mightily to the severe drop in consumer spending. As this chain of events pushed the economy deeper into

---

2   http://money.ccn.com, October 23, 2008.

recession, access to credit for the everyday consumer and the small-business owner became more restrictive for many and completely disappeared for some.

As consumers and small-business owners lost access to credit, they spent less, creating a huge spending deficit in the economy. That deficit created a drop in demand, not a healthy occurrence in a supply-and-demand economy. This drop in demand fundamentally and dangerously weakened the integral structure that holds the whole economy together.

Consequently, a huge drop in consumer spending puts enormous pressure on the supply side of the economy. States with huge deficits cut budgets, governments lay off workers, municipal construction projects cease, housing construction drops, business inventories rise, production slows, corporate cash flow dries up, profits slip, and the unsold housing inventory increases, causing property valuations to drop faster and further. Suddenly, loud crashing noises spread throughout.

In the middle of October 2008, another ripple from the liquidity crisis and the credit crunch rolled over the economy, knocking down another domino—the stock market. This falling domino created panic as retirees, almost retirees, future retirees, investors, corporations, non-profit groups, institutions large and small, as well as state governments and global investors watched wide-eyed as wealth in the many trillions seemingly vanished into thin air, day after day, month after month.

Stock Market Crash – October 2008

On October 10, 2008, the Dow Jones Industrial Average (DJIA) had just reached the bottom of a steady slide that saw the average drop from 10,850 on September 30 to 8451 on October 10. By any measure, this drop is a crash—nearly 2,400 points in 12 days. This precipitous drop came on the heels of the DJIA steadily eroding from just under 14,000 in May to 10,850 on September 30.

A crisis of confidence had been developing slowly. But with the reality and magnitude of the housing collapse, the financial liquidity and credit crunch, and the developing recession openly revealed, that slow erosion of confidence turned into a swift-moving landslide that sent the stock market to levels not seen since the middle 1990s. Volatility punctuated the slide with huge swings intraday and day-to-day. One day, the DJIA would swing in an 800-point range, ending up positive, the next day it would drop 500 points, and the next, it would go up 300. In one two-day stretch, the DJIA dropped more than 1,000 points and the next it went up more than 900. The psychology of fear displaced caution and the crash snuffed out the risk-taking spark that drives greed. The mantra of investors became sell everything in sight, especially financial stocks.

Stock Market Psychology

Actually, this domino became wobbly in January of 2008. That month, the stock market started its steady decline from the lofty heights reached in 2007. Slowly but surely, the market retreated until September 2008. Obviously, the market sentiment had changed from the bullish furor seen in 2006 and 2007, but directional sentiment is different from a major psychological shift. Bull and bear markets come and go, often generating little greed and little fear.

The bear market today is quite different from a directional sentiment; it represents a major psychological shift that may take years to overcome. The market hit depressing lows in November 2008, rallied in December, and then found its way to deeper lows in February and March 2009, followed by a strong rally. Fear is driving this market and greed supports it.

In the October crash and the move lower through November, large institutions such as mutual funds and hedge funds drove the market down with massive selling. Some of this was protective action for clients, while other selling, particularly from hedge funds, happened because of overleveraging during the bull market. Like many financial institutions, the liquidity crisis, the collapse of the commercial paper market, and the credit crunch negatively impacted hedge funds. Many sold depreciated assets to raise capital for loans called in and to cover losses associated with seemingly worthless paper carried on their books. October, November, and part of December 2008 saw massive liquidations from these large institutions, which drove the market down and caused fearful selling from those who envisioned a complete and total market crash. Fundamentally sound, cash-generating companies saw their stock drop in value as much as 50% or more, in some cases.

Ultimately, investors left the market, which turned it over to the traders. Toward the end of January, it had fundamentally become a traders' market with greed as the driving force. The short sellers took advantage of the fear and dominated the bear market, driving it down little by little every day.

Low volume and intraday volatility marked the action of the market.

Then the second crash arrived in February and early March. On February 6, the DJIA stood at 8,280, roughly the bottom of the trading range it had occupied since December. On March 9, it fell to a low of 6,547, a drop of 1,733 points in one month. Real panic set in and the pundits, analysts, and newscasters really had something to sell—the DJIA was headed to 5,000, maybe lower. Everyone seemed so sure, so certain. Fear, fear, and more fear ...

Consumer Psychology

As important as stock market psychology is to the economy, consumer psychology is the superstar. Consumer confidence drives everything day to day, month to month, year to year. Unfortunately, as the engine of the economy, if it stalls, everything else follows suit. This domino resoundingly fell in October 2008, and it has remained low ever since.

The Conference Board's Consumer Confidence Index set a record low in October, plummeting to 38 from 61.4 in September (1985=100). The Present Situation Index fell to 41.9 from 61.1 last month, and the Expectations Index declined to 35.5 points in October from September's 61.5 points.

Fear mixed with a solid dose of prudence drove the actions of the consumer then, and the same psychology is still prevalent. The light at the end of this dark tunnel will appear only when the consumer fully regains confidence and returns to more normal spending patterns.

Something Changed

A clear demonstration of this consumer effect at work is what happened in March and April 2009. Some good news slipped into the daily negativity. Citigroup, Bank of America, Wells Fargo, and JP Morgan announced operational profits for Q1 2009. Fed Chairman Ben Bernanke announced the Fed would take whatever actions were necessary to keep the economy running. GM declined $2 billion of bailout money for March. Treasury Secretary Tim Geithner seemed more confident testifying in front of Congress. Larry Summers, the leading economic adviser to President Obama, started speaking, and both he and the President adopted a more openly sympathetic position toward the business community. The administration started speaking confidently with one voice.

Consumer confidence rose slightly in January and February. The DJIA staged a bear market rally, rising from the low of 6547 back up to 7223 in four days. Fear still dominated, but now a tempered, tiny voice whispered, "Perhaps we have reached the bottom."

Auto Manufacturing

As a domino, this economic problem child began its fall when it bypassed re-tooling to make lighter, more fuel efficient, and less expensive cars, the same type of car that Toyota began manufacturing seriously in the 1980s and the same type of car Toyota, Honda, Nissan, and Hyundai began importing into the United States throughout the 1990s. Instead, American carmakers opted to keep the large-framed, less fuel efficient, and more expensive cars that were primarily sold to Americans in fewer and fewer numbers as the price of gas steadily climbed during the last 30 years.

Putting aside any feelings about saving these mismanaged companies, current wisdom argues two practical reasons for saving these companies. The first is that if they were allowed to fail, up to 3 million more people would be out of work, the supply chain for the industry would suffer a crushing, perhaps fatal blow, and the creditors holding the industry together with monetary "band-aids" would lose billions of dollars, adding more economic misery to a country mired in economic malaise.

The second reason is an historical one. What we learned from World War II is that the dog that ends up on top when the fighting is done is the dog that gets the biggest bone. America's cohesive spirit, righteous determination, and manufacturing capability provided the edge needed to win the war. And when the war ended and America assumed its role as the leader of the free world, manufacturing capability propelled the nation forward on the road (literally) to riches. U.S. innovation, brains, and manufacturing capability brought the country the title of the wealthiest, most prosperous nation that the world had ever seen.

The United States has lost most of that manufacturing base in the last 30 years, but what remains are the American auto manufacturers, survivors of an industry that helped build the nation into what it has become. Losing this last bastion of manufacturing is not only an historical and cultural loss; it is a national security issue. The United States became top dog in WWII because automobile manufacturing plants cranked out more and better-built transport vehicles, tanks, trucks, jeeps, and, most important, spare parts than the enemy could.

The question is can the automakers adapt to the fuel-efficient world dominated by foreign carmakers? Can they make cars that Americans will want, can afford, *and* be fuel-efficient?

Deflation

At the end of all this decline is the specter of long-term deflation. Commodity prices were not immune to the speculation that drove the stock market in 2007. Almost all commodities experienced sharp increases in prices as the bubble inflated, and in most of 2008, commodities seemed to be a safe haven for investors as the impending financial crisis began to unfold. No commodity, though, rivaled the upward climb of oil in 2007 and 2008 and its fall in the last half of 2008. Figure 3.3 tells the story of the rise and fall in the price of oil in this period.

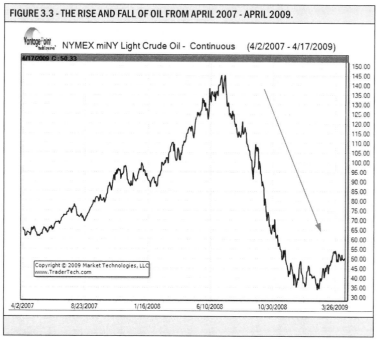

FIGURE 3.3 - THE RISE AND FALL OF OIL FROM APRIL 2007 - APRIL 2009.

If there were just one telltale sign of where we were headed in July of 2008, it would have been the price of oil. On July 11, 2008, the price of a barrel of crude oil futures hit a record high of $147.27. On December 19, 2008, the price of crude oil fell to $32.40 a barrel, the lowest since the global financial crisis began. In mid 2009, it found a trading range between $65 and $75 a barrel.

Housing values have continued to decline, sales of consumer goods, both large and small, are flat or declining, and inflation remains around zero. Gold prices settled above $1,000 an ounce on March 3, 2008. Reaching that height again on February 9, 2009, the price has remained somewhat stable since, fluctuating on either side of $900 since late 2007. The point is that deflation is a legitimate concern; however, with the recent blowup in federal spending, the issuance of trillions of dollars in U.S. Treasury bonds, and the Federal Reserve loaning trillions to the ailing financial sector because it can simply print the money, hyperinflation is a legitimate concern for the future. At this moment in the economic fight, though, it appears the only way to win is to spend our way to victory. Without the American consumer to do the job, the only other entity big enough to help pick up the slack in consumer deficit spending is the U.S. government. Recognizing this, the government stepped up in a huge way.

GOVERNMENT SOLUTIONS

TARP

The first act of fighting back came in the fall of 2008 when then Secretary Paulson asked Congress for $700 billion to shore up the failing U.S. financial system. He received the money in the form of the Troubled Assets Relief Program (TARP) and immediately issued half the $700 billion, plus another $140 billion outside TARP. All totaled, he delivered $490 billion without any strings to some 19 banks.

From October to March, many questioned the wisdom and legitimacy of this. True, lending rates had decreased, and some lending had returned, but overall, the liquidity problems and the credit crunch still existed into March 2009. When Citigroup, Bank of America and JP Morgan announced operational profits in March, many pundits and analysts began to see the wisdom of Paulson's actions and concluded that these actions prevented the collapse of the financial system. Delivering the money to the banks without strings let them use it as they saw fit from a business perspective. Even though some abuse of the monies occurred, and the media and Congress appealed to the populist thought about greedy bankers, it appears, in fact, most all of the money was used for the intended purpose—recapitalization of the incredibly overleveraged banks. It appears that it worked, at least for now.

TALF

In 2009, we now have The Asset-Backed Securities Loan Facility (TALF) that targets triple-A rated credit card, small business, student, and auto loans by trying to thaw the securities markets backed by asset-backed securities. Before the crisis, the asset-backed securities market accounted for about 40 percent of all consumer lending. The money for this program is the second half of TARP, totaling $350 billion.

We do not know yet what the full, remedial impact this program will have on the restrictive consumer-credit market, but it has received positive comments from economists, and it is beginning to show signs it is working.

The American Recovery and Reinvestment Act

The $790 billion "stimulus" bill, as it is called, passed both houses of Congress with a total of three Republican votes. The highly debated act is designed to take up much of the slack in spending for 2009 and 2010. Pro arguments claim it will stimulate the economy in the short term, and it provides money for transitioning the economy to the 21st century. Arguments against it say it does not spend enough overall or that it spends too much on social programs and not enough on "shovel-ready" projects.

Again, not enough time has passed to evaluate the success or non-success of this program, but the Obama administration predicts it will create or save up to 3.5 million jobs in the next three years.

Mortgage Rescue Plan

In July 2008, Congress passed and President Bush signed The Housing and Economic Recovery Act of 2008, legislation designed to stem the rapidly rising rate of foreclosures. Has it worked?

This program has had relatively little success since its inception. Many argue it is too restrictive. Staff from the Department of Housing and Urban Development have said the program has not insured a single loan, and Federal Housing Authority-approved lenders have only closed on 25 loans. The program was designed to help 400,000 homeowners.

The attempt to stem the rising foreclosure rate had no apparent impact in 2008. In fact, December had one of the highest foreclosure rates in history. The foreclosure rate declined in January 2009, but the temporary halt in foreclosures by several major banks played a large part in this decline.

As of January 2009, foreclosures all over the United States dropped by more than 25 percent with the majority of the severely hit states witnessing declines in the quantity of homes reclaimed by lenders. On the national level, completed foreclosures plummeted from 97,841 in December 2008 to 72,694 in January 2009, the lowest number of completed foreclosures since April 2008. Moreover, pre-foreclosure filings, which gauge the future of completed foreclosures, dropped as well to 12 percent from 190,467 in December 2008 to 166,860 in January 2009.

The foreclosure rates in February and March 2009 shot right back up, indicating the foreclosure problem still plagued the economy in a big way.

The number of households threatened with losing their homes rose 30 percent in February from last year's levels, RealtyTrac reported... Nationwide, nearly 291,000 homes received at least one foreclosure-related notice last month, up 6 percent from January. While foreclosures are highly concentrated in the Western states and Florida, the problem is spreading to states like Idaho, Illinois and Oregon as the U.S. economy worsens. The rise in foreclosure filings came despite temporary halts to foreclosures by Fannie Mae and

Freddie Mac and major banks JPMorgan Chase, Morgan Stanley, Citigroup and Bank of America.[3]

In mid-February 2009, President Obama announced his plan to stem the rising rate of foreclosures. The plan went into effect on March 4. It is still too early to tell if this plan has worked any better than the plan implemented in July 2008, but several important differences between the current plan and the July 2008 plan are worth noting.

The first is the tax dollar commitment of the current plan compared to the one in July. The Bush plan committed no tax dollars, while President Obama's plan is a $75 billion effort to stem the rushing tide of foreclosures.

The second is the aggressiveness of the Obama plan. The Bush plan relied primarily on the voluntary efforts of banks to reach out to homeowners who were in trouble. The Obama plan brings together a number of financial regulators and the federally run mortgage giants Fannie Mae and Freddie Mac to deploy a four-pronged approach aimed at helping at-risk homeowners, those facing foreclosure, as well as those already going through foreclosure.

The third is the number of homeowners targeted in the plan. Remember, the Bush plan targeted 400,000 homeowners, while the Obama plan allows for up to 5 million individuals to refinance their mortgages through Fannie Mae and Freddie Mac. It would help 3 million to 4 million homeowners modify their current loans to a more affordable monthly payment level.

---

3   http://cbs5.com, March 12, 2009.

The final difference is the goal of each plan. The Bush plan had the goal of freezing adjustable rate mortgages to slow the rising pace of foreclosures. The goal of the Obama plan is to bring down mortgage interest rates overall by allowing Fannie and Freddie to increase their mortgage portfolio holdings.

Bank Rescue Plan

After much time and deliberation, Treasury Secretary Geithner put forth the details of the bank rescue plan. Although the plan has a variety of complicated components, the centerpiece develops public-private investment partnerships to buy up the toxic assets sitting out there.

Administration officials said the plan deploys $75 billion to $100 billion from the existing $700 billion bailout program for the purchase of bad assets — resources supported by loans from the Federal Deposit Insurance Corp. and a loan facility operated by the Federal Reserve. Under a typical transaction, for every $100 in "bad" mortgages purchased from banks, the private sector would put up $7. The government would match the $7. The remaining $86 would be a government loan guarantee provided in many cases by the Federal Deposit Insurance Corp.

Fundamentally, the government will leverage capital, along with private investors' money, to buy the toxic assets. An auction will determine the value of the assets for sale.

Several large investment firms have indicated an interest in this idea. The upside of this plan is that if the assets go up in value over time, the government will split the profit 50-50 with the private investors. The downside is that if the investments fail to produce profit, taxpayers and the private investors will lose money, but taxpayers will lose 13 times more than private investors will. Because of the problem evaluating the toxic assets, many argue this approach to resolving the problem is the best of all possible worlds. Others argue it is simply prolonging the inevitable collapse of the financial system.

Bank Re-regulation

Congress is drafting regulations that will both prevent (hopefully) further excesses and protect the investor. The goal is to make the system more transparent, not to "over regulate" it, proponents contend. Two proposals that will likely become law would establish a "Systemic Risk Regulator" to ensure that new and old regulations are followed and would put in place a Financial Products Safety Board, much like the Food and Drug Administration or the National Transportation Safety Board. More than likely, critical parts of the Bank Act of 1933 will return to re-erect the wall between banks and other investment companies, and the regulations that constrained the leveraging abilities of banks will surely return.

The idea that some financial companies are "too big to fail" has prompted legislation that will disentangle and break up some of the largest companies, such as AIG and Citigroup. This legislation also ensures that financial companies can never again get so big that a failure on their part can wreck the economy and then hold the taxpayer hostage.

A THOUGHT TO CONSIDER

The government established credit-rating agencies (CRAs) in the 1920s as a safeguard for investors. For decades, investors paid the agencies to evaluate and rate bonds in an unbiased manner. In this downturn, the best of those agencies got it completely wrong. Many gave high ratings to companies that are now on the brink of failure and even higher ratings to the exotic CDOs.

According to internal documents released at a congressional hearing, while rating agencies strenuously defended their independence publicly, some of their top executives acknowledged privately that they faced fundamental conflicts. As one executive at Moody's, a major credit rating agency, put it following an internal discussion on the implosion of the subprime mortgage market, "These errors make us look either incompetent at credit analysis, or like we sold our soul to the devil for revenue." The documents lend credibility to charges that the rating agencies deserve part of the blame for the current financial crisis.

Given this reality, we need to ask, until these agencies are re-regulated, how valuable are they? Consider the following information. Within the world of mortgage-backed securities, (MBSs) and CDOs, CRAs rate on the following criteria, according to The University of Iowa (www.uiowa.com).

1. **The Financial Instrument**

    The rated instruments at the center of the financial crisis include MBSs and CDOs.

2. Institutions Holding the Financial Instruments

A financial instrument's rating affects the credit rating of the investing institution. As of mid-2008, foreign investors held the most MBSs (20%), followed by Fannie Mae and Freddie Mac (16%), and commercial banks (16%). Key CDO investors include banks, insurance companies, pension funds, and hedge funds.

3. The Issuers of the Financial Instrument

Fannie Mae, Freddie Mac and banks issue most MBSs. The top MBS issuers in 2007 were Countrywide, JP Morgan, GMAC, Lehman Bros., and Citigroup. Banks are also the primary issuers of CDOs. The top CDO issuers in 2007 were Merrill Lynch, Citibank, and UBS. The statistics below say everything that needs saying regarding the issue of credibility with the CRAs.

In 2006, 79.1% of an average subprime MBS was rated AAA. CDOs were similar—often 95% of a CDO was rated investment grade.

One has to ask if the agencies were incompetent, blind, or simply corrupt. If they could not (or would not) see what was happening in the derivatives market, one has to also question the regulations that bound them, and to whom was their fiduciary responsibility.

FEDERAL RESERVE

It is important to note that the Federal Reserve is, by legislation, separate from the U.S. government. The Fed is the central banking system of the United States. Created in

1913, it is a quasi-public banking system, which means it is a government entity with private components. It is responsible for the monetary policy of the United States, and its primary responsibilities are:

- to maintain the stability of the national currency and money supply;

- to control subsidized-loan interest rates;

- to act as a "lender of last resort" to the banking sector during times of financial crisis;

- to exercise supervisory powers to ensure that banks and other financial institutions do not behave recklessly or fraudulently, and;

- to print money.

Although the President appoints the Fed Chairman, he or she is supposed to act independently from the political apparatus of the U.S. government. Logic dictates this is an almost impossible task, since presidents naturally appoint those who agree with their economic philosophy.

In this current economic crisis, Chairman Bernanke has exercised all of his responsibilities to help stem the economic downturn. He has lowered the Fed rate to virtually zero, loaned out trillions to banks, and has committed trillions to buying U.S. Treasury bonds and guaranteeing toxic assets. There is some evidence that this effort is beginning to work, as lending between banks seems to be improving and mortgage rates are dropping to record low levels.

The Fed has loaned trillions to banks in this crisis with AIG and Citigroup receiving $210 billion between them. There is some evidence this money is having an effect on stabilizing the largest banks in the financial sector as three of the largest banks, Bank of America, JP Morgan, and Citigroup, reported operational profits for Q1 2009, and Wells Fargo reported a $3 billion profit for Q1 2009, although there remain some questions about the accounting practices to arrive at those profits.

There is ample evidence that Bernanke is working in concert with the Obama administration to re-regulate the banking system to ensure that the reckless behavior of the last 10 or more years does not occur again. He has called for broad new powers to oversee financial markets.

The last responsibility, to print money, is the one many argue will lead to hyperinflation. When the Fed pledges money to the financial sector or buys back its own Treasury bonds (quantitative easing), it alters its balance sheet, which is why many are concerned about future inflation. Simply, too much printed money dilutes the value of all money in the system.

Certainly, the Fed altered its balance sheet when it loaned trillions to ailing banks and AIG. On March 18, 2009, however, its balance sheet took a lopsided hit when Bernanke announced plans to buy up to $300 billion of long-term government bonds, up to $750 billion in additional mortgage-backed securities guaranteed by Fannie Mae and Freddie Mac, and up to another $250 billion in toxic assets elsewhere. The primary goals of this quantitative easing policy are to lower mortgage rates to jump-start the housing market and to help clear toxic assets off the books of ailing banks.

Mortgage rates have dropped below 5%, but only time will tell if pushing down mortgage rates through quantitative easing will lure people back into the real estate market. In the meantime, the government argues that injecting capital into the recessionary and deflationary environment is paramount to a recovery. Inflation is an evil that can be faced after a recovery from the economic mess.

What we all need to be clear about is the intended effect of injecting so much capital into the economy, whether it is through the U.S. government or the Fed. Known as the "multiplier effect," this simply means that every dollar injected into the system moves through the system synergistically increasing the effective value of the original dollar. For example, if $100,000 goes to a building project, the workers, contractors, and suppliers are paid with that money, and then each of them goes out and spends that money for their own purposes and needs. Thus, every dollar given to the project multiplies its effect throughout the economy. This is the expectation of the $790 billion stimulus bill.

One concern of some economists, as well as the opponents of the stimulus bill, is that in the current economic environment people may not spend the stimulus beyond their immediate needs. They may save it for a rainy day. The relative term for this consideration is the "velocity of money," which is mathematically computed relative to the money supply. For our purposes, we can simply see it as how quickly the money moves through the economy or how quickly it is spent.

Again, we cannot know the actual velocity of this injected money until more time passes, but one thing is certain:

There is the possibility for massive economic stimulation, if the money moves through the system quickly.

One final note here is that in the past year, the U.S. government and the Fed have injected upwards of $13 trillion into the economy in one form or another. This total dollar number is one to watch for guidance on future investments, especially the effect on the U.S. dollar and what that means to global financial markets.

CONFIDENCE BUILDING

The ultimate solution to the recession is having the American consumer regain confidence in the economy and the global investor regains an appetite for risk. Consumers must not fear losing their jobs to layoff, losing their home to foreclosure, or losing their way of life to bankruptcy. Consumers must not fear losing their retirement, their life savings, or their children's college education to a crashing stock market. Investors must once again see markets as an avenue for making money.

Given this, the government's ultimate role is to instill confidence with every action it takes and in every speech, every word officials utter in the public realm. This is not to say our officials should sugarcoat our problems. No, they need to tell us straight up the reality of the economy, but they should never talk down or imply we can do nothing to save ourselves.

WHY THIS RECESSION IS UNIQUE

When trying to understand one thing, it helps to compare it to another. Our news media is adept at using this rhetorical technique to explain the economic mess. The problem with this approach is that it does not accurately represent the unique nature of this economic downturn in this time in our history.

In sports, people often compare athletic heroes from different eras to establish the singular greatness of their particular hero. The problem is that comparing the feats of one athlete who played on grass, for example, with one who played on artificial turf cannot answer the basic question of who is the greatest athlete. The reason is the context. The cultural, sociological, technological, and economic context defines the qualitative judging of an athlete. Because no historical era is like another, one will always end up with irreconcilable differences, if one tries to compare the accomplishments outside of contexts.

The same is true for comparing economic downturns from different historical eras. To understand the current economic downturn, it is best to see it in its own context. Then one can look to other economic downturns in other historical eras to find similarities and differences that might further illuminate our own economic problems.

The current combination of economic problems is unique because the historical context is unique, as is every historical context. For example, the Internet has a profound influence on the economy, an influence never before seen in history. Another profound and unique influence on current economic problems is the pervasive and powerful nature of our 24-hour news cycle. Still another is the impact that the global economy has on the economy of any individual country. Still another is today's geopolitical environment, which is like no other time in history. For these reasons, then, generally comparing this economic downturn to other U.S. downturns with the tool of commonality is helpful.

Historically, one thing that all U.S. economic contexts share are the principles of supply and demand. Understanding the principles of supply and demand allows us to understand the basic nature of economic problems, to see that the participants in the previous economic downturns essentially faced the same basic issues. We can then compare their approach to solving supply and demand issues with ours.

Defining and characterizing the whole of a supply and demand economy such as ours is complex, but understanding the fundamentals is actually simple. Basic rules drive all systems, and supply/demand is no exception. Thus, looking at the basic rules and how they apply at any given time in an economy provides a macro-economic view that is quite helpful. Given the above, then, assuming the goal of equilibrium in a supply/demand economic system, the following three general principles always apply:

1. When demand exceeds supply, prices go up.
2. When supply exceeds demand, prices go down.
3. When supply and demand rise equally, one will eventually exceed the other, causing price disequilibrium.

What the U.S. economy is experiencing are these fundamental supply and demand principles at work. Initially, when the demand for housing exceeded the supply, prices went up. Eventually, supply caught up, and prices continued to rise. All three continued to rise together. Here is the fundamental imbalance that caused the housing collapse. As principle number three states, supply and demand cannot rise equally. One will eventually exceed the other. In this case, supply exceeded demand and prices dropped.

Within the housing equation above is another integral player, the banks. A supply and demand economic system relies heavily on credit to keep it growing. Thus, as the demand for housing rose, banks had to keep pace with loan demand to keep the cycle going. To sustain the growth, banks increased their demand for dollars to lend. Banks borrowed dollars to lend, just as their customers borrowed dollars to buy. Thus, demand and supply rose together, finally reaching a state of disequilibrium when the overall demand for dollars overcame the overall supply of dollars and prices dropped.

It is clear to see the self-correcting mechanism in this system. This poses an important question: Is the system inherently flawed? The answer is yes, but not to the degree that it is unworkable. If the system operates without control, the tendency is for activity within the system to generate more ways to make money, ultimately ending in disequilibrium. This is the essence of the boom-and-bust cycle. To control the boom-and-bust aspect of supply and demand, the process must be regulated to keep the activity more in equilibrium. Of course, this opens the debate about how much regulation is necessary to keep the system in equilibrium. Our interest here is not the debate. Instead, the focus is on understanding the economy so we can become better investors.

Now that we see what is common to all other economic downturns, looking to what makes the current situation different is helpful to understanding how we should prepare to invest when the economic recovery begins. To do this, we must understand that the current economic situation is like no other in history.

With our ability to transmit information instantaneously around the globe, decisions and actions occur with unprecedented speed. Financial transactions and news that shape both investments and economies occur, and within moments, the effect is known. The reaction to the effect is almost instantaneous in return, which sparks another set of actions and reactions, and so on.

The U.S. economy links to the global economy in ways unimaginable even 15 years ago. The economic decisions U.S. political leaders make inform the economic decisions other political leaders make because no one country can afford to fall behind another economically. As well, the economic decisions that corporate leaders make have the same action-reaction construction and consequences on the global economy. More people than ever before in history participate in the global supply and demand economy and human behavior by its very nature is variable. In any system, adding more variables adds complexity, which reduces predictability.

Given just these differences, one concludes that, to evaluate economic and, by extension, investment decisions, one needs to incorporate as many variables into an analysis as is possible. Like most things in nature, within that thing is the seed of its own evolution. This is exactly the case here. Computers are the reason information moves at light speed around the globe. Without computers, none of the technology that moves the information would be possible, specifically the Internet, which is the primary medium that carries the information. Thus, the seed is the computer and the evolution is global intermarket analysis, an analytical approach pioneered in the 1980s by my father, Louis Mendelsohn, and transformed into practical use with the release of VantagePoint Intermarket Analysis Software in 1991.

Intermarket analysis is the latest evolution in investment analysis. This analytical approach incorporates global economic and market information with computer-software technology to predict possible outcomes. In short, intermarket analysis incorporates as many global economic variables as possible into its analytical framework. Thus, intermarket analysis is the foundational principle behind our search for data points that will act as guideposts pointing to an economic recovery. Intermarket analysis is also the framework we utilize to formulate our conclusions about potential investment opportunities that will arise when the eventual recovery arrives.

Out of necessity and the need for reality, I have pointed out in some detail the myriad problems the U.S. economy faces. I have avoided any optimism other than to say that the economy will eventually recover. That is all about to change.

In the coming chapters, I will write frankly, reasonably, and optimistically about the economic future. I will point to all the positive reasons why and how the economy will recover. I will discuss the potential future realistically but with a sense of expectation, an expectation that the things that have made this country great and the U.S. economy the most productive wealth producer in the history of the world will begin producing again. I will also take my optimistic sensibility one step further in relation to what I have already discussed in the preceding chapters.

As rapidly as things fell apart for the economy, the reasons stated for why this economic downturn is unique are the same reasons the economy will recover from this downturn more quickly than most pundits believe. To that end, for the first time in this book, I use the word "hope" as part of our outlook—I hope I am right.

CHAPTER

— 4 —

SIGNS OF RECOVERY

It cannot be stated firmly enough that no matter how bad things are now or how bad they might get, the economy and all its associated markets will recover. The issue is not if but when. I will give you my take on what to look for as signs that the economy and the stock market have bottomed and are on their way to an enduring recovery. I make a distinction between the economy and the stock market because, historically, the stock market bottom precedes the economic bottom, sometimes six to nine months in advance.

The first common-sense tenet of any cycle is that before it can go up, it must stop going down. Somewhere in the cyclical process a bottom forms. Sometimes, though, when at the bottom of a cycle, the components of that cycle bang around, moving back and forth in a somewhat turbulent state. Think about it this way. Fill a glass about 1/10 full and swirl it. This is how the elements in a cycle behave at the bottom. At this point in the cycle, we have two foci—one, when has a bottom formed, and two, the force of the swirl.

Lots of swirl produces lots of agitation. Minimal swirl produces minimal agitation. To answer the question of when, *and* to evaluate the turbulence at the bottom when we get there, look to key data points.

KNOWING THE ECONOMIC BOTTOM

Knowing a solid economic bottom when we see it is difficult, to say the least. One reason it is difficult is that in the down part of a cycle, bad news, as I have discussed, is a powerful force. Bad news destroys confidence, and a lack of confidence keeps the cycle going. In December 2008, the heavy spate of bad news from October had played out. It seemed we had become accustomed to the enormity of the economic problems. The only thing that could reinvigorate more confidence loss was more bad news of a different nature, which we got in January.

So, here is the first question to ask when identifying the bottom: Is there more bad news of a different nature coming? Because we can never predict the future with all of its possibilities, we can't know the answer. What we can know, though, is the relationship of good news to bad. If the good news is slowly marching to overtake the bad, then we are getting to a bottom. When it does overtake the bad, a bottom more than likely is forming. This point is important because, as we have seen, minimal amounts of good news helps, but if they are just "green shoots," as Bernanke calls them, they can easily die in a frost of bad news. A steady movement of good news tells us that the economic cycle is getting to a bottom, and more good news than bad tells us when it is at the bottom.

When I say news, I am not talking about analysts and talking heads telling us their perspective. News is hard economic data. To get hard economic data, go to the U.S. government or to a reliable news source. The first news to seek is non-farm payroll data.

THE UNEMPLOYMENT NUMBERS

The Employment Situation: March 2009

Nonfarm payroll employment continued to decline sharply in March (-663,000), and the unemployment rate rose from 8.1 to 8.5 percent, the Bureau of Labor Statistics of the U.S. Department of Labor reported. Since the recession began in December 2007, 5.1 million jobs have been lost, with almost two-thirds (3.3 million) of the decrease occurring in the last 5 months. In March, job losses were large and widespread across the major industry sectors.

Even though the number of unemployed is a lagging indicator, it is the key to forming a bottom. When that number stops increasing and begins stabilizing or decreasing in successive reports, a bottom is forming. However, just as we do when we invest, we should not accept one indicator as the end all. We should confirm what we think we know before we make a definitive judgment. Thus, when the number of unemployed stabilizes, we look to the consumer.

CONSUMER SPENDING

The Commerce Department reported that consumer spending edged up 0.2 percent in February 2009, in line with expectations. That follows a huge 1 percent jump in

January that was even better than the 0.6 percent rise originally reported.

March, April, and May produced similar numbers, more or
less. When unemployment stabilizes and consumers spend at
a substantially improved rate, a bottom is forming. To be certain, though, we should look to some key commodity prices.

COMMODITIES

Copper

Copper is a leading indicator of economic activity. Think
about this. Virtually every electronic product manufactured
requires copper. If the price of copper has stopped falling
and stabilizes or rises, this indicates an increase in demand
for a material widely used in most all manufacturing. It is a
sign a bottom is forming.

Oil

As the economy fell in October and November 2008, the
price of oil plummeted. People drove less. Less demand and
the supply price drops. When the economy showed some
"green shoots" in February, March, and April, the price of oil
climbed back to the $40-$50 a barrel range. By June, the price
of oil climbed back to the $70 per barrel level. When the price
of oil stabilizes in the $65-$75 range, a bottom is forming.

Gold

Historically, investors flee to gold in times of economic
uncertainty. This downturn affirmed what we already
knew. Even though markets experienced the bear rally
in December 2008, the price of gold barely faltered. One
viable interpretation was that further problems were on the

way. They were, and gold climbed above $1,000 per ounce on March 3, 2009. Since then, though, gold has remained in the $900 to $975 zone. Does this mean a bottom has formed? Only confirmation from other signs will provide an answer.

PRODUCT INVENTORIES

Because much of the problems we now face are from a lack of demand in a supply and demand economy, product inventories tell us much about where the economic cycle is. One sure sign of impending recovery is when inventories drop to the point that they can not meet a rising demand. For now, dropping inventories are a good thing.

Gas

Gasoline inventories reveal if people are driving again; if they are, they are spending money on gas. More than likely, though, if people are driving beyond the daily needs of work and family requirements, they are probably driving recreationally, which means they could be spending for other things beyond just gas. If gasoline inventories are decreasing in conjunction with consumer spending rising, this is a good sign a bottom is forming.

Oil

If oil inventories decrease, it means the demand for oil is increasing. Because oil has a vast economic meaning (plastic manufacturing and road building, to cite just two examples), a drop in inventory in conjunction with other signs could confirm a bottom is forming. Keep in mind that, logically, it would seem gasoline and oil inventories should directly correlate; they do not. Sometimes one will drop and the other will rise, or vice-versa. If both are dropping together in a trend, this is a sign that demand is returning, which means a bottom is forming.

Manufacturing, Trade, and Sales

Although these reported numbers (see Figure 4.1) lag approximately two months behind, they are extremely helpful in determining the formation of a bottom. What we look for is a continuing trend.

FIGURE 4.1 - ESTIMATED MONTHLY SALES AND INVENTORIES FOR MANUFACTURERS, RETAILERS, AND MERCHANT WHOLESALERS (IN MILLIONS OF DOLLARS)									
	Sales			**Inventories1**			**Inventories/Sales Ratios**		
	Jan. 2009	Dec. 2008	Jan. 2008	Jan. 2009	Dec. 2008	Jan. 2008	Jan. 2009	Dec. 2008	Jan. 2008
	(p)	(r)	(r)	(p)	(r)	(r)	(p)	(r)	(r)
Adjusted2									
Total Business	1,004,014	1,014,558	1,166,795	1,440,075	1,455,834	1,461,901	1.43	1.43	1.25
Manufacturers3	369,404	375,980	437,643	537,568	541,986	537,497	1.46	1.44	1.23
Retailers	308,461	302,852	343,739	478,280	486,517	504,564	1.55	1.61	1.47
Merchant Wholesalers4	326,149	335,726	385,413	424,227	427,331	419,840	1.30	1.27	1.09
Not Adjusted									
Total Business	920,370	1,060,191	1,086,364	1,427,260	1,436,556	1,451,367	1.55	1.35	1.34
Manufacturers3	335,500	368,574	404,937	534,495	528,015	534,311	1.59	1.43	1.32
Retailers	281,464	354,475	312,020	467,613	480,352	494,118	1.66	1.36	1.58
Merchant Wholesalers4	303,406	337,142	369,407	425,152	428,189	422,938	1.40	1.27	1.14

Unsold Housing

It would seem that, because the housing market collapse is at the root of financial problems, the inventory of unsold homes should be viewed as a primary sign of recovery. The inventory number does help to ascertain where the market is in relation to stemming the rate of foreclosures and to confirm a bottom forming, but like unemployment, it is a lagging indicator. People will only start buying real estate again in meaningful numbers when the fear of losing one's job goes away and confidence in general returns. Our job as investors is not to jump in after things begin moving fast to the upside. Our job is to identify the bottom and set up for the rise. Tracking the inventory of unsold homes helps do this.

RISE IN MANUFACTURING PRODUCTION

Simply, a rise in manufacturing production means inventories have been reduced to the point of satisfaction, and people are going back to work to produce goods, which means more people will spend more money. In this simple scenario rests the seed of consumer confidence. A steady increase in manufacturing production is good news, which will act as fertilizer for Bernanke's green shoots. To continue the metaphor, those shoots will develop a root system that will stabilize and feed the now growing plant. Our job as consumers and investors is to nurture and support the growth, and we will do it if we feel good that we are buying and investing at the bottom of our economic cycle.

CHINA, EUROPE, AND JAPAN

Looking at what is happening in other countries is constructive and insightful to understand what is happening to the United States, as all countries are in this together to one degree or another. As these countries begin their bottoming process, it will provide more confirmation that the market is actually making a bottom. Simply, Europe and Japan have been hit harder than the United States has. The United States entered the recession before the other countries did, so the argument goes that the United States will get out of the recession before they do. If that is true, then bottoms for them will provide solidifying confirmation of a U.S. bottom having formed.

China is a different story, but one that will provide confirmation of the U.S. bottoming process, nevertheless. As an economic power with no debt and a GDP that is contracting, yet remaining positive, the bottom for China is quite different than it is for Europe, Japan, or the United States. When China's economy bottoms (GDP growth stabilizes), we can be assured the United States is at the bottom because countries are now so interconnected economically that one cannot move forward without the other. If China's economy is growing again, it means that its largest trading partner (United States) is importing China's products, which confirms that U.S. consumers are indeed spending again.

FINANCIAL SERVICES AND REAL ESTATE

A sustained recovery cannot truly begin until the financial system is solvent and the rate of foreclosures returns to an average norm. When the government announces the end of the bailouts for both of these industries, we will know that an overall bottom has formed and the new economy is taking shape. Before that happens, though, we can look to data points that will foreshadow that event, putting us in a more positive investment position.

Bank Profitability

Clearly, if banks start reporting operational profits on a consistent basis, it will suggest light but not that the economy is out of the tunnel. Operational profits are important as an indicator of health, but the "books" tell the real tale when all is said and done. Not only do investors want to see profit, they want to see an end to the asset write downs and a substantial reduction in the toxic assets on the books of the major financial institutions. When this happens, profit will have more meaning. As well, it will indicate banks are lending again, which is a critical factor for a sustained recovery.

Bank-to-Bank Lending

The three-month LIBOR indicates credit health on a global scale. Interestingly enough, the LIBOR has remained around the 1% mark since December, way down from its highs of October and November 2008. However, international lending on a bank-to-bank basis is still cold, if not frozen, because confidence is lacking. Until bankers have more confidence that borrowers will not default on loans, they will require the most stringent collateral before lending. In this market of so many banks with bad "books", this makes lending and borrowing difficult. When bank-to-bank lending increases on a regular basis, this will be a sign that the economy is coming to the end of the dark, financial tunnel.

Foreclosure Rate

When the foreclosure rate slows considerably, it is the best sign that the market collapse is subsiding. More than likely, this will coincide with a reduction in the inventory of unsold houses. When the inventory of unsold houses is reduced to a manageable three to six months, we will take this as a sign that consumer confidence has returned to some degree, banks are lending more normally, and the housing market is on the mend.

CATERPILLAR

Many bellwether companies exist and should be watched, but Caterpillar is an important one in this economic downturn. Much like copper (utilized in all electrical components), Caterpillar is the company that supplies the world with heavy-duty construction equipment, the kind used to build roads, bridges, docking ports, infrastructure, and other large-scale construction projects. When this company begins to show marginal improvement in both its bottom line and in its forecast, it is a strong sign that a bottom may be forming or that we are on the upswing.

CONCLUSION

The above data points are primary indicators for assessing a lasting bottom formation in economic activity, but it helps to look to other points as well. Consumer borrowing, consumer debt, and the national savings rate are three. These are interesting data points to watch because we actually hope they will be bad. As in the vernacular of today, "bad" is good.

Even though we as a nation should (and hopefully will) aspire to achieve historically average norms for these numbers, in our current economic situation, the irony is that we need to see borrowing increase, debt increase, and savings decline, much like they have been doing since 1980, give or take a few years. Yes, the deep ironic twist of this reality is almost too much to handle. We need a strong dose of the poison that ails us if we want to recover from the illness we inflicted upon ourselves.

In the end, the most powerful sign of an enduring recovery is consumer spending again. If the consumer returns, even modestly, it would provide a stimulus to the economy more powerful than anything the U.S. government has done and can do. When the consumer returns, we will know for sure that a bottom has formed.

Even though the recession will eventually bottom out, a sustained recovery may take a while longer. As stated earlier, our economic problems are unique because of the confluence of negative economic events unseen in history. Ultimately, even though the recession will end, a sustained, long-term recovery will only come when more is done than mitigate the problems in the real estate and financial sectors. To get back on a healthy growth path, the economy must resolve these debilitating problems, as well as re-regulate the industries to rebuild confidence in these sectors. The good news is that investors will not have to wait for total resolution and re-regulation to begin investing again in either the real estate or stock markets.

KNOWING THE STOCK MARKET BOTTOM

The trading range of December 2008 clearly looked like a bottom, but, as it turned out, it was only the cycle pausing on the way down. The same may be true of the bottom in March 2009.

Like the economic downturn, bad news moves numbers in the wrong direction. Again, it is all about the psychology of fear and greed. A bottom will form only when investors confidently believe a bottom has formed. Remember, a negative potential future creates a negative present and a positive potential future creates a positive present. One sign that investors are feeling more positive and a bottom is forming is when the extreme volatility that has become expected is no longer expected. Again, another "catch-22" is at work here.

VOLATILITY

In October and November 2008, the stock market showed volatility so extreme that it shook the foundation of investors' belief in the whole system. In October, the DJIA swung up and down almost 2,000 points in two days, an unprecedented display of volatility never seen before in history. The precipitous drop on Black Tuesday in October 1929 (350 to 40) compares in shock value, but nothing compares with the breathtaking context of the day-in and day-out volatility witnessed in October and November 2008. The extreme hyper-volatility arose because institutions and hedge funds were dumping and buying as the unfolding liquidity and credit crises affected them and because the panic selling created more fear, even for the "big guys."

Not as dramatically, but the stock market is still volatile in 2009. One big reason is investors, large and small, have pulled their cash to the sideline. Traders command the ebb and flow of the stock market on a daily basis, which causes the up and down fluctuations. Once investors come back, the market will settle down, which will entice more investors to reinvest bigger dollars in the stock market, but this will only happen on a sustained basis when investors are confident a bottom has formed. In effect, when volatility is diminishing, it is a sign that the stock market is forming a bottom.

One thing that should be watched is a return to a more humdrum daily movement in the overall stock market. Humdrum is more telling than rapid rises and rapid falls in valuations. Remember, a sudden rush to new heights is potentially as bad as a sudden rush to new lows. If the stock market goes up quickly, one thing is certain: Profit taking will occur. The stock market, like any other system, always seeks equilibrium, and in today's fast-moving, instantaneous, online trading environment, the attempt to equalize can come swiftly with enormous ramifications.

The degree of volatility described above is a qualitative judgment on my part. I trust my judgment, but even when trust is not an issue, it is still good to look for more quantitative analysis when rating volatility. For that, I turn to two important volatility indexes.

CBOE Volatility Index (VIX)

Look to the VIX for clues about the level of volatility. Simply, when the VIX goes below 30 and remains there, this is a sign that volatility is diminishing and a bottom is forming.

CBOE NASDAQ Volatility Index (VXN)

The VXN points to volatility, or lack thereof, in the technology sector. This is helpful in determining a bottom. Like VIX, if the VXN goes below 30, begin to look for a lasting bottom.

TRADING VOLUME

When the stock market crashed in October and November 2008, one prominent characteristic was high trading volume. In the rally of December 2008, trading volume diminished, and it remained lower than normal in early 2009. When the averages turn up and trading volume begins a gradual resumption to normal or spikes above normal levels on a consistent basis, take this as sign of a lasting bottom.

S&P 500 P/E RATIO

Another sign that the stock market is getting ready to move consistently in an upward direction is the price to earnings ratio of the S&P 500 Index, perhaps the most reliable gauge of stock market activity. Looking to history shows how this number can help us. In the last three big recessions (1975, 1982, and 1990) when the P/E ratio dropped below 15, this indicated an absolute market trough. In these three examples in Figure 4.2, the S&P 500 began a long-term movement in the upward direction.

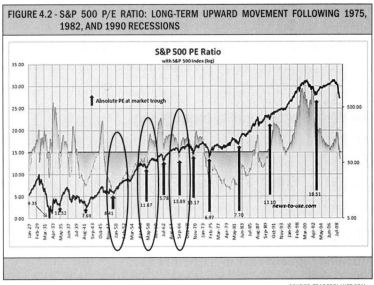

FIGURE 4.2 - S&P 500 P/E RATIO: LONG-TERM UPWARD MOVEMENT FOLLOWING 1975, 1982, AND 1990 RECESSIONS

SOURCE: TRADERPLANET.COM.

As of March 31, 2009, Standard and Poor's reported the non-absolute P/E ratio stood at an incredible high-water mark of 52.62. Until this number comes down quite a bit, the risk appetite for investors buying into the stock market will remain low. When it begins to drop on a consistent basis, take that as a sign that a bottom is forming.

Keep in mind that the stock market bottom precedes the economic bottom by roughly six to nine months. Thus, if you believe the stock market has bottomed, you have a window to begin implementing your strategies. Of all the things I discuss in this book, having a strategy is one of the most important.

DOW JONES TRANSPORTATION INDEX

I discussed the movement of goods at length and how important that is to economic growth. I historically demonstrated the value of transportation in any economy. The Dow Jones Transportation Index (DJTA) is a leading indicator for tracking the strength or weakness in an economy.

The DJTA is the most widely recognized gauge of the transportation sector. It is also the oldest index used today, even older than the DJIA.

The transportation average is composed of 20 stocks that represent the transportation industry. Some of the stocks are FedEx, United Parcel Service, Union Pacific, Ryder System, Burlington Northern Santa Fe, Norfolk Southern, Southwest Airlines, Continental Airlines, Northwest Airlines, AMR Corp., and Delta Air Lines.

When the index reaches and sustains a level above 3,250 that will be an important sign that the stock market has bottomed and that the economy is on the mend.

CHAPTER

— 5 —

DEVELOP A STRATEGY

T he idea that one can trade or invest without some type of strategy is, to put it simply, foolish. It adds unnecessary risk to your investment or trading activities, and it eliminates opportunities that could make you lots of money. When the recovery begins, opportunity will abound, and you should approach those opportunities strategically to improve your edge, which increases the probability of success.

Six basic principles guide the strategic approach generally defined in this chapter.

- Protect and preserve capital, even above making money.

- Begin slowly and pick up as the markets track up.

- Diversify into the greatest opportunities.

- Don't push too hard for the best price.

- Follow the money.

- Cash is king.

PROTECT AND PRESERVE CAPITAL

This principle is elemental, but many people do not consider it in their trading and investing activities. In fact, the brightest investing bulbs on Wall Street did not follow this principle when investing in subprime mortgages, exotic CDOs, and credit default swaps. If their foolishness doesn't drive the point home, nothing will. It is the biggest mistake you can make. If you do not protect and preserve your capital, you will have none to invest.

The fundamental nature of this principle is conservatism. The word implies caution and consideration, and it speaks to removing emotion from the plan. You cannot consistently make money if you invest or trade emotionally, which is why I am pushing you to develop a strategy. A lack of emotion and a conservative approach form the foundation of a solid strategy for investing in the recovery and the new economy that will develop as the economy recovers.

ACQUIRE CAPITAL

To protect and preserve capital, one must have it. In these tough economic times, having capital may be a luxury. If this is the case, then acquiring it is the only option.

To do this, look to your portfolio and evaluate it carefully. You may find that some companies are no longer the same "good bet" they once were. As stated, the economy is changing and that fact may affect the quality of companies in your portfolio. Identify those companies and, as the recovery begins, take advantage of any short-term "pops" to sell them. Do the best you can to get as much cash as you can out of them, but don't be afraid to take a loss on a stock that you believe is ultimately not going to recover, or recover well.

If you have other ways to acquire capital, such as saving money from your paycheck or cashing out investments other than stocks that are no longer needed or will not provide the return you want, do so. Remember, though—and this is extremely important—only use money that will not directly affect the quality of life for you and your family. Do not be in a rush to get in. Be cautious, careful, and consider all possibilities when thinking about acquiring capital.

Leveraging is a possibility for acquiring capital, but the same unbreakable rule applies here. First and foremost, protect you and your family. DO NOT, I repeat, DO NOT over-leverage. The costs and destructive effects of this tactic are evident in the economy. Only borrow what you can afford to lose and only pay what you can afford to pay for borrowing.

If you have some cash, devise a short-term plan to buy and sell quickly. Trade your way to the capital needed for long-term investing. Invest a little in a lot to take advantage of the pops in the market, as they will surely be coming as investors and traders decide where they want to be and for how long they want to be there. In fact, if you don't have much capital, this might be the best way to raise more. Stick your toe in and take your toe out with a little more money each time.

RULES PROTECT YOU

Investing and trading are different animals, although they share similar characteristics. Generally, investing is more for the long term, and trading is more for the short term, but both involve buying and selling to make money. When buying and selling, the highest probability of consistent success comes when rules determine when you buy and when you sell. What those rules are depend on what you are doing in the markets, so you must devise them to fit your needs. But make no mistake, utilizing rules is the surest way to protect and preserve your capital when trading or investing.

BEGIN SLOWLY

Starting slowly is the conservative approach for both short- and long-term investing. As both traders and investors realize the economy and the stock market are on the mend, as in the beginning of a recovery, a flurry of money will flow into all of the markets. This will cause some volatility, as traders will dominate the markets in the early days of recovery. Short-term profit taking will rule the markets in the early days, but this does not mean you cannot participate. In fact, I encourage you to move in when the timing is best, but do it slowly. Here are some things to look for early in the recovery process.

FUNDAMENTALLY STRONG COMPANIES

Fundamentally sound companies beaten down from panic selling are prime targets for making money both short and long term. Strong sectors suffering from the liquidity crisis and credit crunch offer these opportunities. Within those sectors, you will find nuggets of gold in strong companies that have a clearly defined path to growth but, in many cases, are 50% or more devalued. Companies with solid fundamentals in strong growth sectors generally offer stable, long-term growth, but in the recovery market, these companies will have more rapid growth as they return to their previous values.

Another opportunity lies in strong companies that prepared for this downturn ahead of the crowd. The companies that cut costs early will come out of the recession early and strong. Those companies are good bets for the short and long term. They showed managerial foresight, and it will pay off. When business picks up, the lower costs, higher revenue combination will quickly generate higher profits.

COMMODITIES

As the economy begins the recovery process, commodities will respond. Sometimes the response leads the actual recovery, and you can take advantage if you have abundant capital and have correctly identified and confirmed the signs pointing to a bottom forming. More times than not, though, most commodities track the recovery in correlation to the improving health of the economy. As the economy improves, demand increases, pushing supply up. It is as simple as that. Two commodities to track are oil and copper. Even though our economy is moving to energy independence, oil will be around for a while, and as stated earlier, all electronic products utilize copper. In the short term, you can raise capital trading on the up and down movement of commodities.

BROKEN FINANCIALS

As risky as the financial sector is, it is ideal for raising capital quickly. The trick is to be extremely careful in your picks. Look for three things in these stocks:

1. Extremely low price

2. Signs of healing such as making profits

3. Bailouts are over or nearly over.

The rule is get in low and get out quickly with a profit. Do not track the up and down movements waiting for more profit. Buy, sell, buy in again, and sell again is the rule.

Short term or long, the same twofold rule applies in all opportunities. Get in slowly and take advantage of movement. This is especially true if you are looking at long-term positions. Buy incrementally as the stock moves up with the recovery.

DIVERSIFY INTO OPPORTUNITY

This principle orients the long-term investor to fundamental safety and maximum returns within that safety zone, which is conservative.

The stock market dropped so far in 2008-2009 that a full recovery will take some time, and it will be bumpy. In the short term, it will rise fast to a point, and then it will recede again. This cycle will repeat, and over time, the frequency and amplitude of the ups and downs will lessen. In the long-term, it will gradually rise to its former height, and as the new economy kicks in, excitement and optimism will drive the market higher.

To realize the greatest return, both short and long term, diversify into strong sectors to spread the risk and ensure success. This approach is no different from a conservative mutual fund, but because you are making the decisions, you can be somewhat less conservative and more proactive in your selections. One important aspect of this principle is that you should not diversify too widely. One strategic approach is to pick five sectors that are fundamentally strong and demonstrate strong growth potential. Of those five, select three that are the strongest. Of those, pick one that shows the greatest potential and fundamental strength. Between all five, allocate investment dollars proportionately based on your rating.

WATCH THE HORIZON

A conservative strategy is wise, no doubt, but some speculative risk is appropriate, if your strategy is sound from day one, if you are religious about following it, if you have the capital to risk, and if the speculative play is sound, not just a fantastic story. We all know about the "sure thing" that could not fail because the product or service was absolutely essential to our future. For evidence of this, just go back to 2000. Look at those sure bets then that are today, well, how shall I say it, bottom dwellers or extinct.

Look for speculation plays that are not startups or stories. Look for companies:

- generating revenue and profit or near-term profit;
- that are well-capitalized and in little danger of losing the capitalization;
- working in the framework of the new economy;
- diligently developing a product or service on a solid time line;
- with a plan to achieve their goals within a ten-year time frame.

The obvious sectors to watch are energy, particularly solar power and even more specifically, solar cells (Japan), and technology, particularly computer/software applications and robotics. Other strong opportunities exist, and you should track those, but remember, this suggested strategic approach is based on the premise that we are moving into a new economy and that economy will be appreciably and qualitatively different from the one we have been in for the last 30 years or so. This is in our favor, and the door that is opening may very well be a once-in-a-lifetime opportunity for making serious money with a conservative strategy.

FOLLOW THE MONEY

This principle is a simple philosophy that successful investors have relied on since investing began—follow the money. Generally, this is true, but not always, and it deserves a caveat as well. When you follow the money, don't do it blindly just because the flow is strong in a certain direction. For example, had you followed the money into real estate in 2006 or oil in 2008, it is likely you would have lost money, and lots of it. I suggest following the flow of consumer and business money, not investor money, which can be fatal when greed comes into play.

When the recovery happens, and that means consumers are spending again, the money flow will be into areas hit hard in this recession. Specifically, one hard-hit area and, thus, one flow to track is likely to be travel dollars. Consumers will feel relief when confidence returns and the economy moves forward. Travel is one outlet to express that relief, which means hotels, resorts, restaurants, cruise-ship lines, and recreational destinations will all experience a flow of money. Airlines will experience a positive money flow as well, but those companies have a particular set of problems that require exclusion from this part of the strategy.

Another flow of money to track when the consumer feels more confident is discretionary spending on expensive consumer goods, such as high-end televisions, audio equipment, and appliances.

Still another is automobiles, especially automobiles. Confidence will move the consumer toward automobiles, but so will the now generous tax incentives, the dollar savings in fuel efficiency, and the notion that we deserve this after all we have been through. Stocks in fundamentally sound automobile companies will go up. Remember, the entire global automobile industry has been beaten down, which offers tremendous opportunity.

As business caters to the rising demand of the consumer, supply-chain companies will also experience money flows. Some obvious examples are those companies that supply the automobile industry, the hotel industry, and the recreational industry, such as ski resorts.

CASH IS KING

Cash is king. Based on the lessons learned in this economic downturn, I recommend keeping a high percentage of cash in your investment portfolio, at least in the short term. Over time, as profit develops, you may risk more capital, but keep in mind, the two things that should never happen to an investor are a shortage of cash that prevents investing and a shortage of cash if the economy goes bad, and it will. Bet on it.

A THOUGHT TO CONSIDER

My dad taught me the art of negotiation. One element of good negotiating is to get the best price. There is a caveat to this: Get the best price but do not risk losing a good buy. In other words, if the profit you envision is there in the price offered, take it. If you wait for the price to go lower just to increase your profit, you may lose the whole deal. Keep this in mind, as many good deals will present themselves in the coming months.

CHAPTER
—6—

POTENTIAL INVESTMENTS

E conomic recoveries and transitions to new economies present a wide range of investment opportunities. If you are careful about researching and selecting those opportunities, the payoffs can be rewarding. However, just as carefully, you must watch out for those investments that seem "too good to be true." These investments always pop up in such situations because con artists and flim-flam specialists prey on those looking to take advantage of the pending opportunities. The stock market world has more than its fair share of these folks, and with the Internet, these people have a door to reach many millions.

Don't be one of those who fall prey to slick e-mails with fancy graphics and well-written pitches from someone "who once was like you" but is now rich. Or from someone who presents a flawless analysis of current market conditions and then gives you a "hot tip" on a small-cap stock whose price is going to triple in a short time.

Be even more aware of those who have sterling reputations in the stock market world as, without malice or intent, they can be the most dangerous of all. Witness what has happened in the last year, for example. Some well-known names in the stock market world were pushing AIG, REITs, and oil at $140 per barrel. Mostly, these people are not evil nor are they trying to swindle you, although some may be feathering their own nest with the "pump and dump" foolery prominent in a market headed downhill.

The point is that you should rely on your own abilities to find the investments that work for you, in your time frame, and within your pre-defined strategy. Yes, you should listen to "experts," but remember, they are just people who are investing, too. As I have stated before, if you do your homework, understand the economics, and practice safe investing, you probably know as much as they do about how to invest wisely. Their "advice" should be just another piece in your overall pursuit of information that will make you a better investor.

You would also be wise to consider another lesson my father taught me about the business of investing and trading. It is a slight twist to an old maxim, "A bird in the hand is worth two in the bush."

When I first began working with my dad when I was about six years old, he told me the saying above, but he changed it to, "A bird in the hand is actually worth three in the bush." In today's investment and trading world, this new twist has particular value because it generally refers to the idea that, if you have a market investment, the profit from that investment is nothing until you sell it (or buy it, as the case may be). Paper profit is, well, paper profit. It is not real until it sits in your account. That paper profit is the "two birds in the bush." What my dad wanted me to understand is that the "third bird" in the bush might also be worthless, unless you have the foresight to get in on an investment when it is undervalued, not when it has reached its highs. In other words, taking profit in hand has actual value, but taking profit after you have "bought in" at or near the bottom is even more valuable. Look for undervalued assets and buy them.

Now, having just said the above, here are some general areas that I think will offer solid investment opportunities when the recovery arrives. These potential investment areas derive from research, and they, like all advice from others, should just be another piece in your pursuit of information that will make you a better investor. My choices are not definitive, nor are they guaranteed to produce profit.

OPPORTUNITIES TO CONSIDER

In the early part of the recovery, volatility will create a lot of market movement in the indices. Moving in and out of the indices might offer an opportunity to raise capital.

I also like forex as a short-term play. In particular, throughout this economic downturn, the U.S. dollar has held its own against the euro and fared well against the yen. When the recovery comes, consider these two points:

1. With the recovery comes the possibility of hyperinflation in the U.S. economy, given the massive amounts of dollars injected into the financial system.

2. As global equity markets go up, the yen tends to go down. It is likely that between the euro, the U.S. dollar, and the yen, quite a bit of movement will take place.

The Mini contracts are one way to play the opportunities in both the indices and forex.

MINIS

- E-Mini S&P 500 Index
- E-Mini DIJA
- E-Mini NASDAQ 100
- E-Mini Euro FX
- E-Mini Japanese Yen
- Micro FX pairs

EXCHANGE TRADED FUNDS (ETFS)

Exchange-traded funds (ETFs) are a solid way to play the movement in the early stages of the recovery, both nationally and internationally. In fact, consider ETFs as part of your long-term strategy as well.

ETFs are good investment tools because they allow you to trade the wide range of possibilities within an area, which, to a degree, reduces risk. As well, ETFs also save you time. Instead of searching for just the right investment in just the right situation, you can assess a broad range of investments across a wide range of possibilities. Based on what we have learned about the impending recovery and the new economy, I have listed some national and international ETFs that I think are good plays.

- iShares MSCI China

- iShares MSCI Europe

- iShares MSCI United Kingdom

- iShares MSCI Germany

- iShares MSCI Brazil

- Energy Sector SPDR

- Consumer Discretionary SPDR

- Financial Sector SPDR

- iShares Russell 2000 Value Index

- iShares NASDAQ Biotechnology

- Materials SPDR

- PowerShares DYN BLDG & Construction

- Energy Sector SPDR

- Semiconductor HOLDRs

- Technology SPDR

- Vanguard REIT or DJ Wilshire REIT

SECTORS

In my strategy recommendation, I suggested defining your investment allocation according to ranked sectors. I have listed below the sectors I think will do well in both the recovery and the new economy, and have ranked them according to potential investment strength. It is not exhaustive, as so many possible investments exist in a broad range of areas. Keep in mind both short- and long-term goals when choosing sectors.

✔ **Energy**

- *Oil* (short term)
- *Alternative energy*
  - ➻ Parts suppliers
  - ➻ Manufacturing
  - ➻ Utilities

✔ **Technology**

- *Computer*
  - ➻ Semiconductors
  - ➻ Network systems
- *Software*
  - ➻ Enterprise
  - ➻ Artificial intelligence
  - ➻ Web-directed
  - ➻ Security related
  - ➻ Medical
- *Robotics*
  - ➻ Public safety and security
  - ➻ Manufacturing
  - ➻ Medical

- *Nanotech Manufacturing*
  - ➻ Water treatment
  - ➻ Batteries
  - ➻ Computers
  - ➻ Medical

✔ Real Estate

- *REITS*
  - ➻ Commercial
  - ➻ Residential
  - ➻ Construction

✔ High-end Consumer Goods

- *Automobile manufacturers*
- *Appliance manufacturers*
- *Electronics manufacturers*

✔ Travel and Leisure

- *Hotel chains*
- *Resorts*
  - ➻ U.S. and Latin America
- *Recreational lodging*
- *Suppliers of recreational goods*

THE INVESTMENT TOOLS

I nvesting and trading tools come in all sizes and all shapes. Many of them work well and many are hocus-pocus. Many of them are what you create for yourself, such as spreadsheets and technical charts with custom trend lines. For our purposes here, I will focus on just two areas of investment tools—predictive software and social networks.

PREDICTIVE SOFTWARE

I have based all of my analyses in this book on the fundamental premise of intermarket analysis—no market is unique unto itself. In this, the age of the Internet, all markets in the global economy affect one another; to understand a single market, you must account for that effect.

Many predictive software packages are on the market and some are very good ones, to be sure. But none of them utilizes the power of neural networks and intermarket analysis to forecast the development of potential short-term, medium-term, and long-term trends. None of them except VantagePoint Intermarket Analysis Software, that is.

One theme prevalent in this book is technological advances improve the way we do things and, at the same time, that improvement, in all its myriad forms, creates opportunities to make money. VantagePoint is exactly this—a technological advance that has improved how to identify market trends while simultaneously creating an opportunity to make money. The current 8.0 version is an example of state of the art predictive software for investors, but more than that, it is a solid, confidence-building investment tool. The reason it builds confidence is not because it gives you an infallible money-making choice every time you use it; rather, it builds confidence because as an investment tool it forces you to fully develop your trading and investment skills. It does this precisely because it does not give you infallible money-making signals.

You see, VantagePoint only works consistently well for you if you do the work every successful trader and investor has to do: Know your markets, define and implement a strategy, and trade without emotion. If you do not trade or invest doing those things, no software, no matter how good, will do you any good. Good trading and investing is about you and your choices. VantagePoint is an excellent tool, but it is only a tool.

VantagePoint is at the top of the predictive software field for trading and investing. Still, it will improve.

As we move from the old economy to the new one, many things will change for the better. As I discussed in this book, important changes are coming to the software industry. VantagePoint is not immune to this. In fact, Market Technologies will ensure that VantagePoint stays on top of the field. More important, it will ensure VantagePoint continues to serve its customers with a product incorporating the latest innovations in software and global market analysis.

Thus, another suggestion I will make is that in preparing for the investment opportunities coming with an economic recovery, make sure that you are following VantagePoint each day if you are already using it. If you are having trouble making money with it, first look to yourself and then look to see if you are utilizing the software as it best fits your trading and investment strategy. A number of resources exist for you to analyze both yourself and your trading style, not the least of which is that excellent customer service is a phone call away. Another way, which ties into an investment tool that is just now coming into its own, is social networking.

SOCIAL NETWORKS

An article in the April 2009 issue of *SFO Magazine*, "Making Connections: Traders Network Online," succinctly and quite rightly lays out the value of social networking for traders and investors. The opening line sums up a major theme in this book, and it implies the evolutionary aspect and potential influence of social networking on the trading and investment world: "As an environment changes, the inhabitants of that landscape evolve."

As the economy changes, we will adapt to take advantage of the opportunities. One way to adapt is to accept the offering of social-networking sites that cater to traders and investors, and there are more than a few. The *SFO* article references numerous sites and defines what each of them offers. As well, it touches upon another theme in this book:

> *The theory goes that the way things were even up to 2000, the trend of people connecting with and depending on each other online is clearly accelerating. The argument is that it is happening now as a result of basic changes in people, technology, and economics.*

The last word, "economics," ties it all back to what I have discussed throughout this book, and the general meaning ties it back to the notion that we, as traders and investors, need to adapt as things are changing, and changing quickly.

The current and potential value of social networking for traders and investors is captured quite nicely in the following quote from that same article. As it is, it will stand as the rest of what I have to say about social networking and its rising influence in the world of trading and investing.

> *Kristel Messer, a twenty-something business coordinator ... an active and eager student of the financial markets, has been a member of the TraderPlanet community since its test phase. She says the site has been a welcoming scene for those new to trading and feels comfortable bouncing ideas off veteran participants who use TraderPlanet ... a one-stop shop for stock market beginners, professionals, and experts who have something to share.*

CHAPTER

— 8 —

FINAL THOUGHTS

Recessions are a natural part of an economy's ebb and flow. In fact, since 1931, we have faced more than a dozen of them (including the current one). That averages to about one every six years. Although no one can predict when this one will end, we can learn from history how best to deal with these periods. For our own broad edification, and to get a context for the timing of this recession, Figure 8.1 shows you the timing and duration of these recessions, and how the stock market (as measured by the S&P 500 Index) responded. I found this chart to be quite illuminating, to say the least.

One point to take away from the chart is one addressed throughout this book: The economy will recover, and when it does, opportunities to make money will abound.

A second, and quite interesting point, is the time lag between the last two recessions. The current one started in December 2007 and the one before it ended in 2002. One

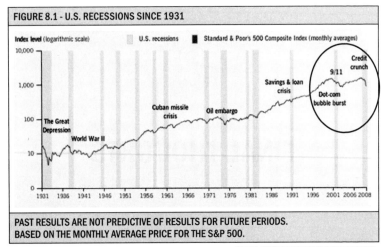

FIGURE 8.1 - U.S. RECESSIONS SINCE 1931

Index level (logarithmic scale)   U.S. recessions   Standard & Poor's 500 Composite Index (monthly averages)

Credit crunch

9/11

Savings & loan crisis

Dot-com bubble burst

Cuban missile crisis

Oil embargo

The Great Depression

World War II

PAST RESULTS ARE NOT PREDICTIVE OF RESULTS FOR FUTURE PERIODS.
BASED ON THE MONTHLY AVERAGE PRICE FOR THE S&P 500.

SOURCE: NATIONAL BUREAU OF ECOMOMIC RESEARCH

take on this is that the latest boom and bust is the last gasp of the old economy.

The short lag between the tech-bubble crash of 2001 and the housing-bubble crash of 2007 reinforces the notion that the old economy and its corresponding unfettered-capitalism philosophy are no longer working. The economy needs a new direction and, interestingly, the tech boom of the late 1990s provided that direction.

Technology, as it has been in all economic transitions, is the foundation of the new economy that is emerging. From the new Internet structure that is coming (Web 2.0) to the developable reaches of the sub-atomic world, technology will change our lives faster and in more ways than at any other time in recorded history. In just the last 30 years alone, technological changes have affected how we communicate, do business, learn, and play. The next thirty years will see the elimination of many diseases, cures for many debilitating afflictions, genetic manipulation of our food, bodies, and pets, inexhaustible energy supplies, perpetual-motion vehicles, commercial space travel. The list goes on ....

Population increases always accompany technological and economic evolutions. Although this will mean new problems to solve, it also means more markets for goods and services, and those markets are developing right now as they find their way out of this latest economic downturn.

The future is always unknown, but that does not mean we shouldn't prepare for what might come our way. This book is an example of preparing for what we think and know is coming—a new economy with tremendous investment opportunities. Get ready ....

ABOUT THE AUTHOR

Lane Mendelsohn has been involved in the financial industry since the mid-1980s, when he joined his father, Louis Mendelsohn, a widely recognized pioneer in the application of personal computers to trading in the financial markets, in his trading software company, Market Technologies.

Lane's progression at Market Technologies from part time helper to Vice President began, when, as a wide-eyed six year old, he started helping his dad on weekends by stuffing direct mail envelopes, copying program files onto floppy disks (yes floppies), and doing general office cleaning. Additionally, as a child and later as a teenager and young adult, he accompanied his father to financial conferences and business meetings with industry participants. As a result, Lane essentially grew up in the financial industry and has known many top technical analysts, brokers, software developers, and money managers most of his life. When he was just fifteen years old he designed Market Technologies' first website presence on the Internet.

Since then Lane has contributed significantly to the company's growing success, as an Inc. 500 company, through his involvement in virtually every aspect of the company's operations including sales, marketing, research and development, trader education, website development, staff recruiting and training, and general management. With focus, determination, persistence, and a passion for the financial markets, Lane continues to approach his responsibilities at Market Technologies with enthusiasm, and particularly enjoys educating traders and providing them with tools for successful trading.

With a guiding hand from his father, Lane learned about the financial industry and entrepreneurship firsthand and developed his business philosophy, which includes the belief that financial education is critically important for success in the financial markets. In 2001, Lane joined the Market Technicians Association as an associate member, and since then has educated thousands of traders, helping them to become more successful in their trading through his expertise with trading software and his knowledge of the financial industry. Lane's vision of providing educational content to traders has resulted in the creation of several popular educational websites dedicated to helping traders become more successful, including his most recent winner, www.TraderPlanet.com, a social networking site that has fostered a growing community of nearly twenty thousand active traders in the first six months since it first launched in January 2009. Through their free membership at TraderPlanet, these traders from all over the world participate in a network of information sharing and on-line friendships fostered through TraderPlanet's commentaries, videos, chats, online news and quotes, product reviews, etc.

In addition, TraderPlanet philosophically represents Lane's commitment to giving back to the community since a major aspect of the website includes a charitable giving component, wherein both TraderPlanet and its members donate money and resources to worthy charities throughout the world. TraderPlanet has been acclaimed by the financial press as an outstanding educational resource for traders, and has attracted many of the trading industry's most knowledgeable technical analysts and traders who contribute valuable daily content for the benefit of TraderPlanet's members.

Lane is not all business, though; or at least not entirely so. His "alter ego" plays in the world of farm and ranch animals as a hobby. Some know him as "Mr. Greenjeans." He enjoys relaxing at his Wesley Chapel ranch raising and breeding Black Angus cattle and taking care of numerous other farm animals including chickens, roosters, Nubian milking goats and even a loveable miniature donkey. Although he does this to relax, he is never one to pass up a good buy or a profitable sell. Sometimes, you can take the man out of business, but you can't take business out of this man.

TRADING
RESOURCE
GUIDE

RECOMMENDED READING

THE VISUAL INVESTOR: HOW TO SPOT MARKET TRENDS
by John Murphy

It's technical analysis made easy! This bestseller shows how to track the ups and downs of stock prices by visually comparing charts—instead of relying on complex formulas and technical concepts. Includes software demo disks, step-by-step instructions for using charts & graphs, and more.

$65.00 | Item #2379

INTERMARKET ANALYSIS: PROFITING FROM GLOBAL MARKET RELATIONSHIPS
by John Murphy

John Murphy on Intermarket Analysis updates the groundbreaking work of a well-known and highly respected technical analyst. A leading educator, Murphy walks the reader through his key tools to understanding global markets and shows investors where they can profit, bull or bear market.

$80.00 | Item #1523697

FOREX TRADING USING INTERMARKET ANALYSIS: DISCOVERING HIDDEN MARKET RELATIONSHIPS THAT PROVIDE EARLY CLUES FOR PRICE DIRECTION
by Louis Mendelsohn

In today's global marketplace, currency values fluctuate every day and foreign exchange is the biggest market of them all, trading well over $1 trillion a day—more than all other markets combined! Master this market that never sleeps, and you could be the big winner. Just to survive in the hottest marketplace in the world, you will have to learn to stay one step ahead of the game.

$19.99 | Item #4183039

TECHNICAL ANALYSIS OF THE FINANCIAL MARKETS

by John Murphy

From how to read charts to understanding indicators and the crucial role of technical analysis in investing, you won't find a more thorough or up-to-date source. Revised and expanded for today's changing financial world, it applies to equities as well as the futures markets.

$85.00 | Item #10239

TRADE YOUR WAY TO FINANCIAL FREEDOM

by Van K. Tharp

One of Schwager's famed "Market Wizards" answers the burning question: What's the one trading method that will bring you trading and financial success? A must read.

$34.95 | Item #4203544

FOR THE BEST PRICE ON THESE BOOKS GO TO -
WWW.TRADERSLIBRARY.COM

TRADING IN THE ZONE: MASTER THE MARKET WITH CONFIDENCE, DISCIPLINE AND A WINNING ATTITUDE

by Mark Douglas

Famed trading coach and "Disciplined Trader" author Mark Douglas provides 5 key steps to successful trading results. Even well grounded traders often fall victim to lapses in judgment and outside pressures that affect stock picking and trading moves. Now, find specific solutions to some of trading's most complicated issues—and learn to triumph over outside influences with the simple exercises found in Douglas' latest #1 seller.

$50.00 | Item #11833

TREND FORECASTING WITH INTERMARKET ANALYSIS

by Louis Mendelsohn

In this groundbreaking new edition, Mendelsohn gives you the weapon to conquer the limitations of traditional technical trading—intermarket analysis. To compete in today's rapidly changing economy, you need a method that can identify reoccurring patterns within individual financial markets and between related global markets. You need tools that lead, not lag. Step by step, Mendelsohn shows how combining technical, fundamental, and intermarket analysis into one powerful framework can give you an early edge to accurately forecasting trends.

$19.95 | Item #5614156

IMPORTANT INTERNET SITES

LANE J. MENDELSOHN | WWW.LANEMEN.COM

Biographical information on Lane Mendelsohn and details on where to find him on multiple social networks.

TRADERPLANET.COM, LLC | WWW.TRADERPLANET.COM

TraderPlanet.com is a financial social networking site that provides individual traders and investors of all skill levels a one-stop destination for financial information and trading tools. TraderPlanet.com is the only financial social networking site that offers its members a full suite of market data feeds, advanced technical analysis tools and exclusive analyst commentary across asset classes, while enabling members to give back to the broader world community with contributions to charitable causes. Designed to level the playing field between institutional and individual traders, TraderPlanet. com's fully interactive, multi-media rich platform is designed to promote the free flow exchange of ideas designed to improve trading strategies and investment performance.

MARKET TECHNOLOGIES, LLC | 800-732-5407
WWW.MARKETTECHNOLOGIES.COM

Headquartered in Tampa Bay, Florida since its founding in 1979 by Louis B. Mendelsohn, with trading software customers in nearly 100 countries worldwide, Market Technologies is a fast growing, Inc. 500, software company and recognized world leader in market forecasting software. Market Technologies researches and develops proprietary trend forecasting and market timing technologies that utilize artificial intelligence applied to intermarket analysis, in order to forecast hundreds of commodity and financial markets throughout the world.

BARCHART.COM, INC. | WWW.BARCHART.COM

Barchart.com, Inc. is a full-service provider of futures, equity and foreign exchange market data and information. Barchart provides a wide range of market data solutions for customers ranging from institutional to retail. From its industry leading website for quotes, charts and technical analysis, Barchart.com, to both retail and institutional data feeds and financial website content for third-parties, and with a heritage dating back to 1934, Barchart has substantial experience in meeting the information needs of the financial, agriculture, energy and media industries.

ACTION FOREX | WWW.ACTIONFOREX.COM

Action Forex provides comprehensive analysis of the forex markets, updated 24 hours a day. Over 40,000 traders receive its free forex newsletter everyday which includes its market overview column Action Insight, classical technical analysis, Candlesticks and Ichimoku analysis, and Elliott Wave analysis. In addition, trade ideas are provided free of charge, together with daily and intraday market bias indicators and support/resistance levels. Its spinoff, Oil N' Gold (http://www.oilngold.com) provides insightful analysis on energies and precious metals markets.

MARKET CLUB | 800.538.7424
WWW.MARKETCLUB.COM

MarketClub is a web-based subscription service which provides research, news, and tools for a wide array of investors and individual traders.

MarketClub's proprietary tools were developed by former floor trader, Adam Hewison and his business partner, David Maher.

SFO MAGAZINE | WWW.SFOMAG.COM

Stocks, Futures and Options magazine has been devoted to the personally active trader for eight years. SFO covers strategies, techniques and resources related to trading as well as specific feature interviews each month from trading experts. Comprehensive, real-life trading experiences of the writers are consistently the most popular articles as they relate to traders. Valuing the future of individual traders, and hence its readers, SFO fulfills its mission as "The Official Advocate for Personal Investing."

SOFTWARE

VANTAGEPOINT INTERMARKET FORECASTING |
800-732-5407 WWW.TRADERTECH.COM

With nearly 80% accuracy, VantagePoint Trading Software gives you the edge you need when trading Futures, Commodities, Forex, Stocks and ETFs.

In today's global economy, markets drive and influence each other. Still, many traders are only analyzing a single market at a time and ignoring related markets that affect that market. Doesn't it stand to reason that taking into consideration related markets in addition to analyzing the target market would significantly impact the accuracy of your market forecasts? Of course it does and that's exactly the type of information VantagePoint customers use to help make their trading decisions.

VantagePoint does not follow trends. It forecasts them! They say "timing is everything" and this is especially true when it comes to trading. This means you need tools that can help you time your trades with high accuracy and precision. Unlike most trading tools and information, VantagePoint does not follow trends. It forecasts them!

TSUNAMI TRADING | 505.918.2270
WWW.TSUNAMI-TRADE.COM

Tsunami Trading Educators, Inc. is a premier trading education and software company. Its flagship software product TsuBot works for any market, any timeframe, and any type of trader. TsuBot analyzes Price, Volume, and Momentum in real time, allowing traders to see the hidden buying and selling pressure in the markets. TsuBot completely analyzes the markets for you, and calls out right through your computer speakers; high percentage trade entries, stops and targets. These trade alerts can be emailed right to your cell phone or directly to your broker for execution. Trading with TsuBot is 100% mechanical, completely objective and low risk.

JAN ARPS' TRADERS' TOOLBOX | 336.282.1237 WWW.JANARPS.COM

Jan Arps' Traders' Toolbox is one of the world's leading providers of technical analysis add-in software tools for traders and investors in the stock and derivatives markets worldwide. Its tools are featured on many technical analysis software platforms, including Bloomberg, TradeStation, eSignal and MultiCharts.

In addition to the large number of unique proprietary market analysis tools developed by Jan Arps' Traders' Toolbox since its founding in 1992, the company has also independently developed programs based on the more popular concepts published by many of the foremost experts in the field of market analysis. A full catalog of products can be seen at www.janarps.com.

Jan Arps' latest book, *A Complete Idiot's Guide to Technical Analysis,* is scheduled to be released in early 2010 by Alpha Books, a subsidiary of Macmillan USA, Inc.

INVEST2SUCCESS | WWW.INVEST2SUCCESS.COM

Invest2Success provides professional investing trading education, training, seminars, webinars, workshops, and events for investors and traders. This includes free information, reviews, comparisons, advisories, trading software, articles, and blogs for stocks, options, forex, futures, and commodities. It also offers weekly stock picks every Monday, and investing trading articles Tuesday through Friday in addition to daily stock market and futures forecast outlook as well as China and India stock market coverage.

Learn More About
VantagePoint Intermarket Analysis Software

□————————————————□

Discover how you can stack the odds in your favor using VantagePoint Intermarket Analysis Software—and its amazing forecasting capabilities. . .

In today's global economy with inter-related financial markets, markets such as Crude Oil, Gold and the U.S. Dollar affect each other and influence other markets. It is no longer prudent for traders to limit their analysis to looking at individual markets in isolation, disregarding what other related markets are doing and how they are affecting the markets that are being traded.

VANTAGEPOINT:

- Forecasts all the major Futures, Commodities, Forex and ETF markets, in addition to individual stocks
- Five neural networks make independent forecasts
- Reports offer detailed analysis on future and past forecasts
- Easy-to-read charts show you what's ahead

Smart traders know that Intermarket Analysis is a crucial piece of the puzzle that needs to be solved to be successful in today's global markets. Now it is not a luxury for traders to have a broad global perspective and the right intermarket analysis tools — it's a necessity. VantagePoint will give you a road-map for your trading showing you what it expects the markets to do. This will give you the self-confidence to pull the trigger on trades that should be taken — and know when to stay out of marginal trades that should be avoided.

VantagePoint anticipates trends—it doesn't just follow them!

VantagePoint was designed by experts who understand what it takes to be successful in today's globally interdependent markets. You need to know what's likely to happen in each market tomorrow, not just what it did today or in the past! Many traders, still using lagging (single-market) indicators get in and get out of positions too late and really don't have a clue about what tomorrow's price action is likely to be. By comparison, VantagePoint uses the pattern recognition capabilities of neural networks to turn traditional, lagging indicators into leading indicators that can give you a clear picture of what is likely to occur in the markets. This will give you a tremendous advantage over other traders.

VantagePoint will place critical predictive information at your fingertips each evening:

- Predictions for hundreds of Futures, Forex, ETF and individual stock markets that are *nearly 80% accurate*
- Anticipated trend direction for the next two to four days
- A forecast of the next day's high & low
- The strength of the trend
- A heads-up on whether the market is expected to make a top or a bottom within the next two days

Plus. . . VantagePoint is quick and easy to use

- VantagePoint is ready to use when you receive it. All you need to do is download daily market data each day off the internet and run VantagePoint. All the heavy lifting intermarket analysis is done for you.
- You do NOT need to know anything about intermarket analysis or neural networks.
- You don't even need to know anything about programming. Unlike other complicated trading software programs, VantagePoint is easy to use and lets you focus on trading instead of getting distracted by the complexities of the software itself.
- The Daily Update function within VantagePoint automatically processes VantagePoint's five neural networks, which then generate

their forecasts for the next day's trading. All you do is compare the Daily Reports (or charts) for several target markets to see which markets offer the best trades to take the next day. The process takes only a few minutes from start to finish.

What more do you need to be successful?

Discover the power of this amazing software program—and start stacking the odds in your favor today. Call us toll free for full details.

Industry Pros, Real Traders, & Product Reviewers are Raving about VantagePoint

▲ ▲ ▲ ▲ ▲ ▲

"Intermarket analysis, or how different markets react and relate to each other's price moves, has never been more important in trading markets than it is today. Louis Mendelsohn is a pioneer in the field of intermarket analysis and his Vantage Point software is a valuable trading tool that will help traders of all markets—from beginners to experienced—extract profits in today's more complex and volatile global markets."

—Jim Wyckoff, Author, Technical Analyst

"Louis Mendelsohn's synergistic approach to trading puts together what many traders know intuitively about the interrelationship of markets in a global marketplace. His software tools quantify these relationships and produce a series of analytical indicators that give traders a timely edge in today's fast-paced markets. As a pioneer in applying the power of the personal computer to trading, Mendelsohn provides insights about combining single-market technical analysis, intermarket analysis and fundamental analysis into practical trading techniques where the whole far exceeds the sum of the parts."

— Darrell Jobman, Author, Technical Analyst

"I've known Lou since the '80's and he's one of the pioneers in the industry. I strongly recommend his products."

— Joe DiNapoli, Author, Technical Analyst

"[Traders] won't suffer from the traditional lag problem of moving averages as it uses predicted values."

— Investor's Week Magazine

"Any user who adheres to the advice in the manuals should quickly recoup their outlay. Highly recommended."

— Investor's Chronicle

"[VantagePoint] provides a signal when a trend may change, sometimes days before it becomes evident with moving averages."

— Futures Magazine

"I tested the index accuracy for all 13 ETF markets and found the index to be accurate anywhere from 77% to 84% of the time – right in line with Market Technologies' claim."

— Stocks & Commodities Magazine

STUDYING MARKETS AND TRADING ...
A NEVER-ENDING JOURNEY

Lane J. Mendelsohn,
Founder, TraderPlanet.com

Now a new trading portal called TraderPlanet (www.TraderPlanet.com) gives traders a source of fresh fundamental and technical analysis information daily as well as many trading education features to help move the trader down the road of more successful trading. Markets are changing constantly every day and every minute, as anyone who has observed recent events can attest. What you read in newspapers and magazines can become outdated quickly, and traders need current information and data to succeed.

But TraderPlanet is more than just a one-way conduit of current news and information directed to users. It is a new social networking experience for traders that provides them with plenty of interaction with other traders

Want to talk to a corn farmer in Iowa or a sugar cane grower in Brazil or a banker in London? Somewhere on this planet someone may want to share their views with you, and TraderPlanet.com's goal is to facilitate those connections wherever traders are located. The global community is now a local community, and TraderPlanet.com is designed to get you acquainted with your trading neighbors.

Now, TraderPlanet.com is not going to guarantee you instant market knowledge and trading success. Many traders feel almost "naked" if they attempt to trade a market when they know little about the fundamentals that affect it. You'll still have to know all of the details about the market

❝ *TraderPlanet has helped me develop my investment strategy by blogging, which is the best way I can imagine to keep a rolling journal. The trading community's comments on my investment ideas really give important feedback about complex ideas.* ❞

Grant Stern

and with top trading analysts and experts – blogs on a variety of topics, chat rooms, trading contests, sentiment surveys and a new gauge of market opinion, the TraderPlanet Indexes for eight market areas. And there are even "My Planet" personal pages for photos and details you may want to share with other traders.

Got a question and looking for an answer about a product, trading strategy or whatever else is on your mind? It is quite likely that there's someone else out there on this trading planet who has been wondering the same thing or is willing to share their experience to help you out.

Join Now at
www.TraderPlanet.com/bookoffer

you are trading, the influence of weather, the timing of key economic reports, the potential head-and-shoulders top and all those other things that make for an informed trader.

But wouldn't you feel more comfortable trading if you had access to current news reports and expert commentaries and could tap the views and opinions of others in the trading community around the world? And do all of this for free?

TraderPlanet.com is a web site where, as its motto says, traders are likely to gravitate in the future.

TRADERPLANET®
WHERE TRADERS GRAVITATE

Marketplace Books is the preeminent publisher of trading, investing, and finance educational material. We produce professional books, DVDs, courses, and electronic books (ebooks) that showcase the exceptional talent working in the investment world today. Started in 1993, Marketplace Books grew out of the realization that mainstream publishers were not meeting the demand of the trading and investment community. Capitalizing on the access we had through our distribution partner Traders' Library, Marketplace Books was launched, and today publishes the top authors in the industry—household names like Jack Schwager, Oliver Velez, Larry McMillan, Sheldon Natenberg, Jim Bittman, Martin Pring, and Jeff Cooper are just the beginning. We are actively acquiring some of the brightest new minds in the industry including technician Jeff Greenblatt and programmers Jean Folger and Lee Leibfarth.

From the beginning student to the professional trader, our goal is to continually provide the highest quality resources for those who want an active role in the world of finance. Our products focus on strategic information and cutting edge research to give our readers the best education possible. We are at the forefront of digital publishing and are actively pursuing innovative ways to deliver content. At our annual Traders' Forum event, our readers get the chance to learn and mingle with our top authors in a way unprecedented in the industry. Our titles have been translated in most major world languages and can be shipped all over the globe thanks to our preferred online bookstore, TradersLibrary.com.

VISIT US TODAY AT:

WWW.MARKETPLACEBOOKS.COM & WWW.TRADERSLIBRARY.COM

This book, along with other books, is available at discounts that make it realistic to provide it as a gift to your customers, clients, and staff. For more information on these long lasting, cost effective premiums, please call us at (800) 272-2855 or you may email us at sales@traderslibrary.com.